Pictured on the front cover *(clockwise from top left):* Rainbow Pastel Parfait *(page 236),* Jiggly Banana Split *(page 148),* Sloppy Joe's Bun Buggy *(page 38)* and Oven-Baked Chicken Parmesan *(page 64).*

Pictured on the back cover *(from left to right):* BLT Cukes *(page 102)* and Smilin' Cookies *(page 220).*

ISBN-13: 978-1-4127-2346-6
ISBN-10: 1-4127-2346-9

Library of Congress Control Number: 2005934377

Manufactured in China.

8 7 6 5 4 3 2 1

Microwave Cooking: Microwave ovens vary in wattage. Use the cooking times as guidelines and check for doneness before adding more time.

Preparation/Cooking Times: Preparation times are based on the approximate amount of time required to assemble the recipe before cooking, baking, chilling or serving. These times include preparation steps such as measuring, chopping and mixing. The fact that some preparations and cooking can be done simultaneously is taken into account. Preparation of optional ingredients and serving suggestions is not included.

contents

Cooking for Kids

Many kids are picky eaters, often preferring sugar over good nutrition. Some prefer variety while others can eat the same foods for days on end. And many children choose junk food and fast food over fruits and vegetables. Then there are the requests for classroom treats. Plus, every kid wants a cool cake to make his birthday special. No wonder cooking and baking for kids can be a challenge!

Cooking for Kids Bible is here to help. You'll find many great tips to encourage your kids to try new flavors, ways to add nutritious foods to meals, and loads of clever suggestions for classroom treats. Discover better fast-food choices and ways to improve after-school snacks. Plus, there are fabulous ideas for easy-to-make birthday cakes, fun party food and on-the-go snacks. Best of all, you'll find the guidance you need to teach your kids to prepare kid-friendly recipes. You'll also learn how to make kitchen rules that keep kids safe while they work in the kitchen.

Cooking for Kids Bible features a collection of more than 180 kid-pleasing recipes for quick and easy weeknight meals, fabulous after-school snacks, healthy recipes, and silly recipes sure to entice the pickiest eaters. There are recipes for birthday cakes, such as Slinky the Snake and Carousel Cake—plus recipes for your child's next party. You'll find spooky ideas for Halloween get-togethers, fantastic recipes for classroom parties and morning treats for sleepover guests.

Whether you're looking for ways to change your kids' eating habits, ideas for birthday cakes, party foods or classroom treats, or guidance for teaching kids to cook, you'll find it all in this must-have book. Show your kids how special they are with silly snacks, unique birthday cakes or tasty meals with fun foods.

Off to a Good Start

Food is definitely one of life's great pleasures, but when it comes to feeding children, it can also become a huge challenge. Parents have the power to pass on a lifetime of healthy eating habits just by making good choices for their children when they are young. As these early choices turn into lifelong preferences, research shows that many adult health problems can be avoided.

Toddlers: Between 12 and 24 months, most toddlers enjoy new foods. This is a great window of opportunity for introducing different types of fruit and vegetables. At the same time, toddlers have relatively small stomachs, so there is little room to fill up on empty calories. Serve sandwiches on whole-grain bread, limit high-fat snacks and be sure juices are 100 percent juice, not just sugar-flavored water. However, toddlers are just beginning to establish their independence and making their own food choices. As long as you place nutritious choices on their plates, you can encourage toddlers to choose what to eat and how much.

Finger foods are not only fun at this age but also are necessary to eliminate choking hazards. Try cutting French toast into basic shapes, slice cooked carrots into "pennies," cut cheese into triangles or bake meat loaves in mini muffin tins. Serve your children whole milk up until they are 2 years of age—they need the extra fat for proper brain development. After that, you can switch to low-fat or fat-free milk. Over the next 3 years, a child's overall fat intake should be gradually reduced to 30 percent of calories, the same guideline that applies to adults.

Preschoolers: Preschoolers should continue to build on the healthy habits that began earlier in life. Foods rich in calcium and protein are important to include as they fuel rapid physical growth. Simple meals, prepared with healthy food, will be most easily accepted. Take advantage of preschoolers' natural curiosity and continue to present new food items. Limit the amount of sweets—sugar adds lots of calories without beneficial nutrients and contributes to tooth decay and obesity.

Elementary Schoolers: School-age children spend many hours away from home and are influenced now by pressure from friends and television advertising. Set a good example of healthy eating and serve nutritious foods at home, then be a bit more relaxed about food choices away from home. Younger school-age children do not need adult-size servings of food, but as the years progress their food intake will rise as puberty approaches. Sports and other organized activities may also increase appetites. As they learn about the human body in school and how food is used, let them get involved in menu planning and grocery shopping.

Preteens: Busy preteens will experience even more freedom in their food choices away from home. Active boys can eat an enormous amount of food (and empty calories), but they still need to fulfill basic nutritional needs. Girls may become concerned about dieting and body image at this time. Trendy coffee drinks contain caffeine as do tea, cola and many other soft drinks. Too much caffeine can cause jitteriness as well as insomnia if consumed too late in the day. Remember that preteens still need the tradition and rituals involved in family meal time. Use this time to reconnect and handle school or family issues at another time.

Techniques for the Table

In order for children to develop a healthy, positive relationship with food, parents need to make the family meal table a happy table. Communication and socialization are just as important menu items as meat and vegetables. While certain childhood challenges can threaten to turn the dinner table into a battleground, a few simple techniques can ease the stress on everyone.

- Small children have small stomachs, which means they need to eat less at a meal but snack more often during the day than adults. A large plate loaded with food can seem overwhelming. Let them fill their own plate from the healthy choices you present, as long as they select three different items.

- Encourage kids to sample new foods. The food may need to be presented up to 15 times over the course of several months before it is accepted. Try new foods similar to ones they already like. For example, substitute banana slices for the jelly in a PB & J sandwich. If your child likes mashed potatoes, try mashed sweet potatoes and then move on to cooked carrots. In this way, the new food already seems somewhat familiar.

- Sometimes it is the texture of a food that is unappetizing rather than the flavor. Try a raw, crunchy version of a vegetable instead of cooked. Some vegetables can be finely chopped and added to soups, chili, casseroles, meat loaf and hamburgers. The same technique can be used to hide fruit in muffins, pancakes or ice pops. Why not start a new family tradition and turn one night a week into "Try a New Food Night"—everyone, including the adults, has to try at least one bite.

- Get children involved in either growing a vegetable garden or visiting an orchard so they can see where food comes from. Or, let them choose a recipe from the "Kids in the Kitchen" chapter, beginning on page 270, and help them prepare it.

- Kids are all about fun, so why should their food be boring? Serve tuna salad in an ice cream cone or soup in a colorful mug. Place meatballs on popsicle sticks so they can eat them like lollipops. Form pizza dough into their initials. Sail a banana boat across a sea of blue gelatin. Many children love to experiment with different dips and dressings. Yogurt makes a great dip for fruit while low-fat salad dressing or a bit of melted cheese may make vegetables much more inviting.

- Some parents worry that their child is not eating enough even though he is growing at a normal rate. Forcing children to "clean their plate" may lead to eating disorders down the road and these dinnertime confrontations will only escalate into more serious battles. Most children can regulate their intake for their own bodies. They will not allow themselves to starve and they also know when they are full.

- Some children develop food jags, eating the same few foods day in and day out. Difficult as is it may be, the best course of action is to make sure the foods they do consume are as nutritious as possible. As long as other options are available and you periodically encourage them to break out of their routine, kids will move on when they are ready. Allowing food jags to be a source of arguments can result in kids using their eating patterns as an attention-getting tactic.

Mealtime should be relaxed and as stress-free as possible. Try to eliminate distractions, such as television, and use the time to reconnect as a family. A family meal is not just a time to nourish the body, it is also an important time to socialize. Avoid arguments over what children are eating (or not eating).

Snack Attacks

Growing bodies require large amount of nutrients and choosing the right snacks can help fill in the missing gaps of a child's daily nutritional needs. Snacks also help keep energy levels high and prevent overeating at mealtime. The perfect snack should actually be like a mini-meal: a small amount of carbohydrate along with some protein and a little fat. A few good examples are crackers with cheese or peanut butter, graham crackers with milk, or fresh fruit and yogurt.

It is best to offer a wide variety of snack options and let children make their own choices. Guide them in the right direction by keeping healthy snack choices at their eye level either in the refrigerator or in cabinets. "Grab and go" snacks can include pretzels, fat-free crackers, fresh fruit, fruit cups packed without added sugar, fat-free frozen fruit bars, whole-grain breadsticks or rice cakes. Snacks that need some preparation include cut-up fruit and vegetables either in a bowl or on skewers, or trail mix made from cereal, seeds and dried fruit. An easy way to control portion sizes is to transfer pretzels or

crackers from a family-size bag to individual sandwich bags. (See page 16 for additional healthy snack suggestions.) Keep in mind that if children graze or snack constantly throughout the day, they will not develop an appetite for meals. Plan on offering snacks at least 1 to 2 hours before a meal; this will take the edge off hunger without spoiling the appetite.

As grade-school children become involved in organized athletics and team sports, it is important to provide energizing snacks either before or during a game. Bananas, bagels, oranges, pretzels and low-fat granola bars are all easily digested and provide complex carbohydrates. Encourage your child to drink water or sports drinks before, during and after the game to prevent dehydration.

Remember that all foods can be part of a healthy diet if eaten in moderate amounts. Chips, cookies and candy should not be completely banned; instead, save these treats for special occasions or once-in-a-while treats.

Meals on the Run

Fast-Food Choices: With today's busy lifestyles, sometimes a quick trip to a local fast-food restaurant is the only option. The good news is that many healthier options are now appearing on the menu besides the standard burger and fries. New choices include grilled chicken sandwiches, fruit or fruit and yogurt, salads with low-fat dressing and low-fat deli sandwiches on wheat bread. The list of least healthy items includes chicken nuggets, French fries, milkshakes, fried fish, double burgers or chicken sandwiches and any kind of "special sauce" or mayonnaise.

It's fine to order the kid's meal, especially when the toy is the latest must-have, but make some substitutions. Milk is a better choice over the empty calories of soda and fruit is more nutritious than high-fat fries or a milk shake. If your child simply must have the less healthy options, put the guilt on hold and balance out the rest of the day with choices that are as healthy as possible.

Restaurants: Moderation is the key when eating at sit-down restaurants. Since portions are usually large, either split an entrée or bring leftovers home for the next day. Skip fried and breaded items and look for broiled, baked or roasted options. Pasta dishes, such as spaghetti and meatballs or ravioli with tomato sauce are good choices. Ask for sauces and dressings to be served on the side. If you want to end the meal on a sweet note, order just one or two desserts for the entire family to share.

Road Trips: Snacks are a great diversion on a family road trip and, with some preplanning, can still be fun and healthy. Freeze bottles of water for instant ice packs and fill the cooler with fresh apples, individual bags of baby carrots and packets of string cheese. Make trail mix with a combination of dried fruits, nuts and whole-grain cereal. Hard candy, gummy bears and animal crackers are non-messy treats and popular kid-pleasers.

School Lunches: Many schools serve hot lunches that are high in fat and sodium, often due to limited facilities and budget constraints. Try to limit these meals to a couple of times a week and become more

creative with "brown-bag" lunches from home. Instead of a sandwich, try a meat and cheese kabob, cheese or deli meat wrapped around pretzel rods or breadsticks, or a thermos of soup or chili. Add a cup of yogurt in place of milk or include a low-fat dip for veggies. Graham crackers are a good low-fat dessert. (See page 16 for other school lunch suggestions.) Add a fun surprise with a sticker or a joke and create your own "happy meal." Involving your child in preparing lunches increases the odds that they will be eaten.

The Power of Television

Children are easily influenced by television advertising, which unfortunately, is usually focused on sweetened cereals, fast foods and snacks. Sports heroes and movie stars only increase the appeal of these foods in young minds. Help your child become a savvy consumer and discuss the power of advertising. Show them an example of how the food on TV never looks as good "in person." Explain why you choose not to purchase certain food items and be firm in your decisions.

Television affects not only young minds, but young bodies as well. Obviously, the more time children spend sitting in front of the TV, the less time they spend in more active pursuits. Physical activity is a key component of a healthy lifestyle and a simple trip to the playground or a game of tag is a perfect way to burn energy and ward off excessive weight gain.

Navigating the Grocery Store Aisles

A few simple ideas can turn a necessary chore into an enjoyable learning experience for your child. The key is to keep children busy and involved in the process. Preschoolers can go on a "treasure hunt" for items that are specific colors or shapes. Older children can match items on the list to coupons and keep a running tally of savings. Play games—guess the weight of six apples or potatoes and then use a scale to see who is the closest. Hand over some of the decisions and let your children choose a shape of pasta or flavor of yogurt. Make sure everyone, including the kids, shops after eating rather than before. Junk food looks much less tempting on a full stomach.

Introducing Junk-Food Kids to Healthier Eating

You're probably thinking healthier eating is an idea that just won't work with your kids. After all, they love their chips, cookies, popsicles, pizza and soft drinks. It would seem too much of a battle to make changes. Well, maybe not. First, you need a simple definition of healthy and nutritious. There's a lot of information available that explains what adults need for healthy eating, but very little guidance for parents trying to improve their kids' eating habits. In the following section, you'll find suggestions for healthful foods to add to your children's meals, nutritious snack ideas and ways to get picky eaters to try new foods and flavors.

The Healthy Six

Healthy foods fall into six groups: fruit, vegetables, whole grains, meat, dairy products and mono- and polyunsaturated oils. These are foods that spell good health and healthy weight; they contain valuable vitamins and minerals that everyone needs to feel good. Adding more of these to the family's meals is an important step in healthier eating.

Fruit: Children should eat a variety of fruit during the week—fresh, canned, frozen or dried. Just be sure to look for canned fruit packed in juice rather than a sugary syrup. Juice counts too. Since juices have less fiber than fruit, go easy on them and avoid serving sweetened juices to your kids.

The United States Department of Agriculture and the Department of Health and Human Services, in their 2005 Dietary Guidelines, suggest that a child between 5 and 10 years of age who gets 30 to 60 minutes of exercise everyday should consume 1½ cups of fruit each day.

Vegetables: A great rule to follow when choosing vegetables is to select them in a variety of colors. Dark green vegetables, such as broccoli and spinach, and orange vegetables, such as carrots, sweet potatoes and butternut squash, are all rich in many nutrients and high in fiber. Tomatoes and red and yellow bell peppers round out the rainbow of choices; these favorites are high in vitamin C. Beans provide a great deal of fiber—occasionally try adding black, kidney or pinto beans to a dish. Lentils, split peas and chick-peas are flavorful options. Legumes contain valuable protein and fiber while being low in fat. By eating a variety of vegetables every week, your child has access to a wide variety of valuable

| Grains | Vegetables | Fruits | oils | Milk | Meat & Beans |

Tip
To learn more about the 2005 Dietary Guidelines, go to the United States Department of Agriculture web site at www.mypyramid.gov.

nutrients. Plus, vegetables are low in calories and high in fiber.

The 2005 Dietary Guidelines make the following serving suggestions for vegetables:

- Girls 3 to 6 years/Boys 3 to 5 years: 1½ cups per day
- Girls 7 to 9 years/Boys 6 to 8 years: 2 cups per day
- Girls 10 to 18 years/Boys 9 to 11 years: 2½ cups per day

Whole grains: Whole grains offer many benefits over refined grains like white flour and white rice. Whole grains are loaded with important nutrients and fiber, making them a good substitute for half of the refined grains in your diet. The 2005 guidelines suggest 5 to 6 servings of grains per day for children between the ages of 4 to 11. Half of those servings should be whole grains. Choose brown rice, whole-grain cereals, whole-grain breads and whole wheat pasta. You might even consider trying less familiar grains like bulgur, barley and quinoa for a change of pace. A serving is 1 slice of bread (1 ounce) or 1 ounce of cereal or ½ cup cooked brown rice. Package labels can guide you with specific serving sizes.

Lean meat and substitutes: Protein is important for children's growth. Elementary schoolers need about 5 ounces of meat, poultry or fish daily. Limit high-fat choices like hamburgers, hot dogs, sausage and fried chicken, and substitute leaner cuts prepared without frying when possible. One egg, ½ cup cooked dried beans, 1 ounce of cheese and 1 tablespoon of peanut butter are equal to 1 ounce of meat.

Dairy products: Milk, yogurt and cheese provide calcium for strong bones and teeth. The low-fat versions are good choices.

Preschoolers need 2 cups of dairy products every day and elementary schoolers need about 3 cups.

The Not-So-Healthy Four

Sugar, saturated fat, salt and refined grains should be eaten in moderation. Replace some of these in your family's meals with the healthy six. Do it gradually. If you don't make a big deal out of it—just a small change today and few more in the weeks to come—kids will more likely accept the changes. The goal is not to eliminate all fat, sugar and refined grains, but to replace some of them with healthier choices. Here are some tips for making it easier.

Fat: Fat is not all bad. Our bodies need some fat for energy and to make it possible to absorb the fat-soluble vitamins A, D, E and K. No one can deny that fat adds flavor and juiciness to food, but many kids eat more than their bodies can handle in a healthy manner.

There are three main types of fats: saturated, monounsaturated and polyunsaturated. Too much saturated fat can possibly lead to weight gain, if a person is eating too many calories. It can also cause an increase in LDL molecules, the "bad" cholesterol in the blood stream. Saturated fat can be found in red meat, poultry, dairy products and oils made from palm and coconut.

Monounsaturated fats have a positive effect on the body by lowering the number of LDL molecules. Examples include olive, canola and peanut oils, olives, avocados, most nuts and peanut butter.

There are two types of polyunsaturated fats: omega-6 fatty acids and omega-3 fatty acids. Omega-6 fatty acids, which are the primary component of corn, sunflower, soybean and cottonseed oils, when eaten in large amounts, can decrease the "good" cholesterol and raise blood pressure. Omega-3 fatty acids tend to lower blood cholesterol. Omega-3 fatty acids are found in fatty fish like salmon, trout and tuna, canola oil, walnuts and dark green, leafy vegetables.

Choose lean, low-fat or fat-free meat, poultry and dairy products when possible. Hydrogenated shortening or trans fatty acids are commonly found in processed foods like cookies, crackers, cakes and snack foods. Reduce your family's dependence on these foods by eliminating as many as possible and encouraging them to eat more fruit, baked snacks and low-fat dairy products instead. Homemade baked goods made with oil, butter or margarine low in trans fat are believed to be healthier for you than foods baked with hydrogenated shortening or products high in trans fats.

Choose healthier fats when cooking. Monounsaturated (olive oil) and polyunsaturated (canola oil) fats are better choices for sautéing. But the calorie load on a gram of any fat is quite high, so it is important to limit dietary fat, even the healthy kind. Trim meat and poultry of excess fat. Choose grilling, broiling, baking or roasting, instead of frying, when cooking.

Sugar: Americans eat too much sugar, which is believed to be one of the causes of obesity. Reducing sugar and its various versions like high-fructose corn syrup, honey and pancake syrup in your child's diet is a healthy decision. Replace some of the sugar in your kids' diets with fruit, a healthier way to satisfy a sweet tooth.

Salt: Consuming excessive salt may lead to increased blood pressure in some people.

One of the greatest sources of excess sodium is processed foods. When children's diets are high in sodium and salty foods, they tend to develop a taste for salt that can last the rest of their lives. Limiting children's access to processed foods and salty chips might prevent this from happening.

Refined grains: Refined grains are the white flour that we bake with and the grain found in processed foods such as cookies, cakes, white bread, some wheat breads, crackers, bagels and pasta. White rice is also a refined grain. The 2005 food pyramid from the USDA recommends that children include two to three servings of whole grains every day. Whole grains are richer in nutrients like zinc, vitamin E and fiber. Look for whole grains in dry cereals, oatmeal, whole-grain breads, brown rice and whole wheat pasta. Whole grains are more nutrient dense, meaning that they are packed with important vitamins and minerals.

Tips for Changing

- **Set a good example:** Young children often mimic what they see, so parents should eat healthy foods. Let children know that you love the flavor and juiciness of a fresh peach. There's no need to push the "it's good for you" message. Let them discover that message in the classroom and share it with you.

- **Get out of the rut:** It's important for everyone to eat a variety of foods. Avoid eating the same dishes repeatedly. Adding variety to your meals can spark an interest in new foods for your children and provide a source of a wider range of nutrients.

- **Change the pantry:** Having ready access to sugary, salty and high-fat snacks makes healthy eating even more difficult. Gradually replace some snack chips with low-fat pretzels or baked chips. Instead of buying the normal week's supply of chips and cookies, buy fewer and smaller bags of these high-fat items. Instead, keep a supply of healthy alternatives on hand.

- **Don't use chips as bargaining chips:** Using food as a reward for good behavior or good grades, or taking away food as a punishment, puts too much emphasis on the importance of food and can lead to eating issues later in life.

- **A little sleight of hand:** Try adding fruit, vegetables and whole grains to favorite recipes. Add carrots or broccoli to your family's favorite chicken casserole. For kids that are resistant to vegetables, finely chop nutrient-dense vegetables like red peppers, broccoli, cabbage and spinach (or grate carrots) and add them to foods like meatballs, meat loaf, burgers, pasta sauces and casseroles. Use brown rice and whole wheat pasta for some dishes. Try adding fruit to desserts. Top ice cream with fresh peach slices, angel food cake with strawberries, or plain cheesecake with fresh fruit. Gradually, your kids will accept other changes, such as fruit or fruit and cheese for dessert.

- **Take it slowly:** Changing eating habits doesn't need to happen overnight. Make changes gradually over months and the process will go more smoothly. This week add an extra serving of fruit to daily menus; next week add an extra vegetable serving and serve fruit for dessert one night.

- **Drink water:** Substitute water for some of the soft drinks and fruit juices your kids consume. Not only is water calorie-free and inexpensive, it's also a better choice for rehydrating active kids.

- **Turn eating fruits and vegetables into a game:** To encourage people to eat more fruits and vegetables, The National Cancer Institute began promoting the five-a-day program a few years ago—eating 5 servings of fruits and vegetables a day. The 2005 Dietary Guidelines from the USDA has increased that number for children to 6 or 8 servings per day, depending on a child's age. This may seem like a lot of servings, but remember that a serving is usually ½ cup. Choose a number that will give your kids a goal. If your kids struggle with eating 3 servings of fruits and vegetables a day, then make the target 5 servings. You can always raise it later once five-a-day becomes a habit. Why not turn this into a game for young children, complete with a chart to track progress and rewards? Choose rewards such as family outings or activities or a new book.

- **Give kids some control:** Kids need to feel they have some control over the foods they eat, so involve them in the decision-making process. Ask them to help you make a list of healthy on-the-go snacks or lunch choices. If decision making is a challenge for them, let them choose between two or three options, such as an apple, grapes or yogurt.

- **Encourage your school to help:** Discuss healthy options for lunches and vending machines. Suggest food-oriented lesson plans for younger children. Day-care providers can help by providing healthy snacks. Toddlers and preschoolers are willing to accept new foods when presented in a relaxed environment.

Teaching children a healthier lifestyle is a great gift that, hopefully, will put them on the path to a long, healthy life. Early lessons often stay with kids. If you have toddlers, start them off right, but never assume it's too late. Introducing older children to new ideas, foods and flavors can be a success. While this book encourages nutritious eating, it doesn't suggest eliminating any food group, such as sweets. Life and eating habits are all about balance.

Introducing new foods and flavors: It's not unusual for children to be suspicious of new dinner offerings. Try some of these tips to encourage your kids to taste new foods:

- Add a small amount of a new food to a dish they like or offer a new vegetable, such as broccoli, topped with cheese sauce.
- Give a new dish a silly name.
- Let your child help you prepare a new dish; encourage him or her to try a new food while you're working together in the kitchen.
- Keep making nutritious foods available until your children are willing to taste them.
- For more adventuresome kids, introduce the one-bite rule: everyone has to have one bite of a new food before rejecting it. Any time you serve a new food, put only a small amount on your children's plates. A large amount can seem overwhelming. If, after tasting the food, they don't like it, then remove it from their plates.
- Handle the introduction of new foods in a calm, reassuring way. Avoid making a big deal out of it. And *never* insist that your child eat everything on his plate.

School Lunch: Lunches served in schools may not include many healthy choices. If this is the case with your children's school, limit them to one or two cafeteria lunches a week and pack lunches other days. Encourage children to choose a brown-bag lunch from a list of options and keep food on hand for as many of the options as possible. Or, suggest that older kids make the list and add to it.

Healthy Snacks

- Fresh fruit: apples, bananas, strawberries, peaches or grapes
- Unsweetened applesauce or fruit cups
- Peanut butter on whole-grain crackers with banana slices or raisins
- Fat-free pretzels or baked chips
- Celery filled with peanut butter, pimiento cheese or flavored cream cheese
- Salsa with baby carrots, broccoli florets, yellow bell pepper strips or baked chips
- Reduced-fat cheese and low-fat crackers
- Reduced-fat yogurt
- Low-fat milk

- Whole-grain breakfast cereal with low-fat milk
- Hard-cooked eggs
- Graham crackers and fat-free fig bars
- Homemade oatmeal-raisin cookies are a more nutritious choice than packaged cookies or homemade chocolate chip cookies. Sneak in a little wheat germ for extra nutrition. No one will know it's there.
- Fruit smoothies made with low-fat milk

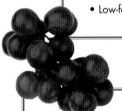

Healthy Lunches

- Kabobs: Roast beef chunks and cherry tomatoes with a light mustard sauce; roasted chicken chunks, red bell pepper chunks and cucumber slices with salsa; strawberries, cantaloupe and pineapple chunks; reduced-fat cheese chunks, cherry tomatoes and low-fat ham rolls
- Reduced-fat cheese and crackers
- Peanut butter sandwiches on whole-grain bread with banana slices or grated carrots
- Egg salad sandwich made with light mayonnaise on whole-grain bread
- Tuna salad with light mayonnaise, celery and mandarin oranges served with whole wheat bread sticks or crackers
- Vegetable, tomato or chicken noodle soup in a thermos
- Corn, celery and red bell pepper side salad with light salad dressing; add black beans and chicken to make it an entrée

- Chicken, celery, and grape or mandarin orange salad with light mayonnaise
- Chicken and green bean salad with light Italian salad dressing
- Hummus with whole-grain bread sticks
- Cheese quesadillas made with fat-free flour tortillas, reduced-fat cheese, bell pepper strips and chopped spinach
- Lettuce and tomatoes, cucumber slices, spinach or avocado slices and turkey or fat-free ham sandwiches on whole-grain bread
- Whole wheat rotini pasta salad with chicken, tomatoes, cooked broccoli or green beans
- Baked corn chips dipped into taco filling mixture made with lean ground beef or turkey and topped with fresh chopped tomato

It's Not All About the Food

Food is only one component of a healthy life style. The other is daily exercise. This will be much easier to implement if you make it fun. Some suggestions follow:

Make exercise a family activity: Bike riding, ice skating, basketball on the driveway and hiking are all fun family activities. Encourage your kids to make suggestions or become involved in planning a special outing.

The importance of sports: Encourage your children to become involved in sports. Organized sports can teach important life skills, like team skills. They also help kids learn to follow instructions and improve coordination. Children who are not competitive may not do well in team situations. They should try individual sports such as golf or tennis, or activities like swimming or horseback riding.

The grandparent factor: Get grandparents involved. They can encourage kids to be more active in sports or exercising. Active grandparents can include grandchildren in their activities. Whether it's swimming, golfing, tennis or bowling, it gets kids moving. Older kids can encourage a grandparent to start a daily walking routine. Let children plan a nature hike for their more active grandparents; this special time will be remembered for many years to come.

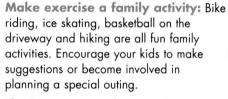

It's Party Time!

What's more exciting for a child than the thought of a party—especially one of their very own! Whether it's a birthday party, slumber party or Halloween party, kids really enjoy entertaining their friends. Food plays a big part in most kid parties; sometimes it's only a birthday cake and other times the food can be planned around a specific theme. *Cooking for Kids Bible* offers a selection of easy-to-prepare but spectacular birthday cakes, fun food ideas, breakfast foods for the morning after the slumber party—plus, weird and scary foods just perfect for Halloween.

Birthday Parties

Birthday parties at home: One of today's popular trends for birthday parties is to hold them at a kid-themed restaurant or activity center, but that can be expensive. You can actually plan a perfect party at home with minimal muss and even less fuss. Entertaining at home allows the freedom to tailor the party to your guest of honor and even get them involved in the planning.

Timing is everything: Hosting your child's birthday party on his actual birthday is not necessary and just puts pressure on you. Instead, choose a Saturday or Sunday close to the birthday for a party with friends. On the birthday itself, celebrate with a small get-together for immediate family only—a special dinner featuring your son or daughter's favorite foods, a cake and gifts. What kid wouldn't like two parties and receiving gifts twice?

Once you've chosen the day, figure out the time. Generally, birthday parties work best in early or mid-afternoon. Younger kids (ages 4 to 6) tend to get tired and cranky by the end of the day, and older kids (ages 7 to 10) tend to become hungry as the afternoon rolls on. If you're serving a meal along with the cake and ice cream, that won't be a problem, but if picky eaters and food allergies run rampant on your guest list, you might want to plan your party to avoid mealtimes.

Most important, however, is how long the party should run. Many parents find that 90 minutes is enough time to feed and entertain a group of young party-goers. But if the kids are 8 or older and you have interesting activities planned, a 2- to 3-hour event may be worth considering.

However you schedule the party, be sure to note the event's start and end times as well as meal plans on the invitation, so your guests and their parents know what to expect. Mail or hand-deliver invitations 2 to 3 weeks in advance. Request an RSVP rather than regrets only. Otherwise, you won't be sure all the invitees actually received the invitation.

The guest list: A common rule of thumb is to plan the guest list based on the birthday child's age plus one: five guests for a 4-year old, ten guests for a 9-year old, etc. This rule serves parents well and makes each passing year increasingly special for the birthday kid. Of course, to avoid hurt feelings, many parents choose to invite the child's entire class, or at least the kids of the child's gender. Do what you're comfortable with— just make sure that if the entire class is invited, that no classmate is missed when the invitations are sent. Have at least one other adult to help you for small parties and several to help supervise a large group of children.

Ages and stages: The key to throwing a great party is understanding the age of those on the guest list. Lucky for you, you have a live-in example: the birthday child. But if you need a refresher on how kids at various ages interact, check out the following information.

4-year olds: Thanks to day care and preschool, most kids this age are at ease with social situations and are eager to take part in activities like singing, coloring or simple games. Some may need a little more coaxing. For children in this age group, make it clear that parents are encouraged to stay for the party. Have some adult finger foods on hand; for instance, cheese and crackers, veggies and dip, and salsa and chips.

5-year olds: One of the best ages for a party! Five-year-olds tend to be fairly independent and put a lot of heart into whatever is going on around them. They respond well to organized activities and attack simple skill games with gusto.

6-year olds: Kids are a little more competitive and rowdy at this age. Ward off hurt feelings by offering both winner and participants prizes for the games. Allocate more money for party favors for these kids—it's all about what's "mine" at this age. It's a great idea to write names on goody bags to help them keep track of their stuff. Make sure you have enough help to supervise these active kids.

7- and 8-year olds: Giggle central! Boys and girls in this age group tend to blend well, but you may hear the first requests for "girls only!' or "no girls allowed!" Let your child help determine the guest list. No matter who's there, these kids love to crack jokes, get silly and laugh about everything. Inspire them with goofy activities like fill-in-the-blank word games and high-energy games such as relay races and tag.

9- and 10-year olds: Maturity has officially set in—or so the kids believe. Children this age can be very particular, so let the birthday child take the reins in planning the party. Decorations, menu, prizes and games will be chosen with a discerning (and trend-conscious) eye; single-gender parties will probably rule and cliques may form. Make sure no one's left out by organizing team-oriented games like a scavenger hunt or low-key group activities. Sleepovers are great for this age.

The little extras: It's important to keep the party safe, simple and special. To keep kids safe, clear the party zone of breakables or dangerous items. If the party guests are preschoolers, put tape over the bathroom door lock so little ones don't accidentally lock themselves in. Shut doors to rooms that are off limits, or tape streamers across doorless entryways to prevent kids from wandering out of bounds. Be prepared to answer parents' questions. They may have concerns about adequate supervision, acceptability of movies or games, or pool safety.

To keep the party simple, designate one room for games and presents and another for food and crafts unless the group is small.

If you can hold any part of the party outdoors, do! Kids love the festive feel of a picnic, and you'll love using a hose to clean up. However, even if sunshine is predicted, don't trust the forecast completely; have a back-up plan ready in case of rain.

Once you've got safety and simplicity in the bag, it's time to make this birthday bash really special. Set the stage from the beginning by decorating the entrance to the party with balloons, streamers or lights.

Everyone will feel the excitement of party central. Plan a low-key activity that kids can dive into, one by one, as soon as they arrive, to help them feel comfortable immediately.

Add special touches whenever possible. Keep fidgeting to a minimum during serving time by covering the table with butcher paper and placing crayons at each place. Small toys and paper cups filled with treats work well, too. Taking photos of the birthday child with each guest or giving each guest a gift bag or a specially decorated cookie—any one of these small efforts goes a long way toward delighting young guests and making wonderful memories for your son or daughter.

Halloween Parties

In recent years, Halloween has become a bigger and better holiday. No longer is it just costumes and "trick or treating," but now Halloween parties are common. If you're a busy parent with little time, patience or pennies to spare, the thought of organizing a party will have your spine tingling. *Cooking for Kids Bible* offers ideas to help you and your kids throw a delightful and frightful monster mash that will have everyone talking.

Make it a family affair: Halloween is one time when everyone enjoys the same kinds of silly and scary site gags, spooky decorations and creatively named food, like Dripping Blood Punch, Mummy Dogs and Green Meanies. That makes Halloween parties ideal for all ages. The older your kids the scarier the decorations can be, but for little kids make it fun rather than spooky.

The whole family can help plan the festivities. It's a great opportunity for kids and

adults alike to exercise their imaginations. Include a creative friend or two when you find your creativity lagging. If you have school-age children as well as toddlers, set up two party rooms, one with scarier decorations and more challenging games for the older kids and one with silly, fun games and decorations for the little ones. You'll need extra adults to supervise the divided group.

Choose a date: Although monsters prefer the dark of night, kid guests are happy to party anytime. If the weather permits, an outdoor party is one afternoon option. When planning a Halloween party for both children and adults, evening is a good choice—it gives you more opportunity to do scary decorations and games.

Don't forget the invitations: You can buy or design your own invitations. Plan to send them 2 to 3 weeks in advance since this may be a busy time of year. Be sure to include date and time of the party and ask for RSVPs at least 1 week before the party. Follow up with those who don't respond. When it comes to kid parties, the only thing worse than running out of food is not having a gift bag for every guest. Let guests know if a meal or light snack will be served or if a scary movie will be shown.

Set a spooky scene: At Halloween, atmosphere is everything. So it's almost impossible to go over the top on decorations. Don't settle for just cobwebs and spiders. Get creative. And don't forget the music; the right sound effects are essential. You can buy a tape or CD of recorded Halloween songs and sound effects, but it's even more fun to create your own customized sound track.

When planning decorations, start at the front door with pumpkin lights and a scary door decoration. Decorate the walkway or

porch with luminaries with cutouts of scary faces, spiders or witches. Add a jack-o'-lantern or two to the mix.

Halloween Luminaries

Buy brown paper bags or plain orange craft bags (7 to 10 inches wide and 10 to 16 inches tall). Draw a design or a word on each bag. Or, spell out a message by printing one letter on each bag. Slip a small cutting board inside the bag, then carefully cut out the shapes or letters with a sharp utility knife. Tape a sheet of tissue paper of computer paper inside the bag covering the design. Add enough sand or kitty litter to the bag to allow the bag to stand upright. Place a small votive candle in each bag and light them just before your guests arrive.

Establishing a theme for your party will help you focus on appropriate decorations. Witches, wizards, ghosts or spiders and bugs are all good choices. Or, if you're short on planning time, keep it really simple and plan a scary movie night with appropriate food; add a few ghostly lights, goblins and spider webs to complete the decor.

Create a witches' lair with a bubbling cauldron, black hats and hovering broomsticks hanging from invisible fishing line. To create fog in the room, place dry ice in a large pan in the corner of the room. If the dry ice is on the floor, the vapor/fog from it will stay near the floor. A small fan will circulate the fog. Always wear protective gloves, break the dry ice into several pieces and use tongs when handling the ice. Periodically add hot water to the pan to create vapor. **Important: only adults should handle dry ice and only use it in a well ventilated room.**

Food is important: Serve a variety of food, both sweet and savory dishes. It can be as simple as some snack mixes, cheese and crackers, and drinks, but it's fun to have a few clever and creative choices. A small

selection of Halloween recipes begins on page 260. Look for Halloween food ideas every fall in magazines on the newsstand or at the grocery check-out counter. Just be sure to give everything a scary or silly name and crudely write the name of each dish on a place card. Serve guacamole and name it "Green Slime." Or serve a bowl of string cheese and call it "Slithering Worms." If you stain the cards ahead of time by dipping them in strong tea, then dry them, they will look old and weathered.

Plan the activities: This is one party that begs for activities to keep kids' imaginations fueled. Plan games, activities and action for every minute of the party. Halloween is the one time when old and young alike let down their inhibitions. You'll find that even shy and self-conscious guests will be more apt to enter into the fun and have a good time if you provide structured activities. For many kids, their fireman or princess costume provides them some anonymity or gives them courage they never thought they had.

Howling Good Party Ideas

- Tell ghost stories by flashlight
- Hire a magician or fortune teller
- Have a costume parade
- Dance and sing to wacky Halloween music
- Bob for apples
- Carve jack-o'-lanterns (older children and adults)
- Act out a shadow play behind a white sheet
- Have plenty of disposable cameras on hand so everyone can take pictures
- Play Halloween-oriented charades
- Plan a scavenger hunt for a mixed group of children and adults

Slumber Parties and Sleepovers

Most kids love to have their friends sleep over. When the guest list changes from one best buddy to four friends, suddenly you have a party to plan. The thought of planning a slumber party may give you a few sleepless nights, but it doesn't have to. First, allow yourself enough time to plan, because the many details of a slumber party take time to organize. Give yourself at least a month for all the arrangements. If you want to stage the party as a follow-up to an activity such as a baseball game, bowling or a concert, you may need additional planning time. Keep in mind that parents often have safety concerns about sending their child to spend the night at someone's home; with careful planning you'll be able to provide answers that will reassure most parents.

Children as young as 5 can do well at a slumber party. But others may not be ready for several more years. To ease young children into this childhood ritual, try a pajama party in which guests arrive at 7:00 dressed in their pajamas and return home by 8:30 or 9:00 in time for bed.

Guest list and invitations: The general rule for number of guests for an overnight party is to take your child's age and divide by two—three guests for a six-year old and five or six guests for an eleven-year old is about right. If you make your own invitations, base them around some planned activity. Send them out 2 to 3 weeks before the party. Requesting RSVPs is a must.

Be specific about the activities you have planned. Parents of guests will want to know that you plan to let your son and his friends sleep in a tent in the backyard or that they will be starting the evening at the local bowling alley. If you plan to show a movie or two, include the title on the invitation. Besides listing the start time of the party, be sure and indicate what time kids should be picked up the next day.

Friday nights are sometimes a better choice than Saturday night. Kids are often more tired on a school night, insuring that they may be able to get to sleep a little earlier. Plus, Sunday mornings may be more difficult to coordinate around church activities. If some of the kids have sports practice or games on Saturday, ask their parents if the child has any special pregame food needs.

Activities: Even if your preteen daughter wants to spend the evening gossiping with her guests, it's a good idea to plan some backup activities. Having a movie or two on hand is always a good plan.

Boys' Sleepover Activities

- Camp out in a tent in the backyard
- Play touch football in the backyard or basketball on the driveway
- Plan a pool party
- Learn magic tricks
- Show a documentary on dinosaurs followed by a dinosaur trivia contest
- Go to a golf driving range or batting cages
- Play board games
- Plan a sports trivia contest
- Race battery-operated cars
- View the stars with a telescope
- Make your own pizza

Girls' Slumber Party Activities

- Create small scrapbooks
- Learn beading
- Paint designs onto t-shirts
- Decorate picture frames
- Capture memories with disposable cameras

- Plan a spa night with manicures, pedicures and makeup
- Play music trivia
- Play charades or Pictionary
- Plan an ice skating or pool party

Safety: Parents will have more concerns about allowing their children to attend an overnight party, so be prepared with answers about party details. Common concerns center around adequate supervision at your home and at off-site activities, acceptability of movies and activities, and suitability of the party menu if their child has food allergies or diabetes. If you're a single parent, you may get even more questions. Make arrangements for a trusted friend to step in if you need to deal with an emergency. Resist the urge to invite a friend over for company because entertaining can distract you from your young guests.

Be prepared if a child becomes uncomfortable or frightened. Take aside any child that is new to sleepovers or new to your child's group and let him know that he can come to you anytime if he changes his mind about staying overnight. Make sure you have emergency numbers for all parents.

The little extras: Instead of trying to find beds for everyone, have guests bring their sleeping bags and arrange them in the family room or living room. A younger (and jealous) sibling can disrupt an older child's party.

Plan a special activity for him or her, such as dinner out with his grandparents or a sleepover at his best friend home.

Have an assortment of books on hand in a quiet corner for those guests who need a few minutes to chill. If the kids plan on watching a movie, encourage them to climb into their sleeping bags for the viewing; with luck some of the kids will drift off to sleep. Light the way to the bathroom or give the kids small disposable flashlights. For early risers, set out cereal, bowls, spoons and glasses and have plenty of milk and orange juice on hand.

Food: Sleepovers usually include dinner or snacks with a special breakfast the next morning. If planning time is limit, take the kids out for a pizza dinner or pancakes the next morning. Or, gather the kids in the kitchen to help prepare pizza, cookies or snacks. They can also help with breakfast the next morning.

Classroom Treats

Whether you volunteered to be a room mom or just offered to bring the treats one day, deciding what to make can be a challenge. But with a little planning, classroom parties and celebrations will be fun for kids and easy on busy moms like you.

Popular treats: Make your party a spectacular success by bringing the treats kids love most. If you're not sure what those favorites are, survey teachers, students and parents to discover the most popular goodies. Here are some suggestions:

- Beverages such as punch with sherbet or ice cream and fun, fizzy drinks
- Snack mixes
- Cupcakes and cookies
- Fruit cups
- Pudding cups
- Fresh fruit, such as apples and oranges

Serve more than the kids: Be sure to check with the teacher to determine the number of servings to prepare. Plan for a few more than the actual head count and always allow extra for staff and parents. The principal, room assistants and parent helpers often attend class parties.

Fuss-free party tips: Decorative or party-themed plates, napkins, fancy straws and disposable utensils not only create a festive atmosphere but also make cleanup a breeze. Even the simplest snacks served on decorative plates add fun to the celebration.

- Think small sizes when selecting paper party goods. Child-size utensils and plates make snacks easier to hold and eat. And, small cups and plates help control serving sizes.
- When party time is short, package and serve snack mixes or cookies in themed goodie bags for easy-to-serve treats.
- Bring food storage bags to pack up leftover treats.

Tip

For a last-minute treat, ask each student to bring a box of his favorite snack—cereal, dried fruits, miniature crackers, pretzels or marshmallows. Put each ingredient in a separate bowl. Add serving spoons and give each student a cup to mix their very own crunchy mix.

Better food choices for kids: Party food can be delicious and nutritious at the same time. Here are some suggestions for easy ways to reduce fat and sugar and still serve tempting treats:

- Serve snack cakes or cupcakes without frosting; moist cakes don't need frosting. Sprinkle with powdered sugar for a festive touch.

- Serve muffins which are lower in sugar and sometimes lower in fat.

- Make small cookies, mini cupcakes and muffins. Sometimes one small cookie or cupcake is the perfect size snack for little tummies. It also reduces waste.

- Prepare a decorative platter with an assortment of cut-up fruits and vegetables or reduced-fat cheese and crackers.

- Incorporate shredded or mashed fruits and vegetables into cookies, cakes and muffins whenever possible. Shredded zucchini or carrots, applesauce or mashed bananas add moistness but less sugar and fat without sacrificing flavor.

- Serve savory treats like mini sandwiches, roll-ups and dips with vegetables.

Special Diets

Ask the teacher about school policies and special dietary needs of the children. If there are food or beverage restrictions because of diabetes or food allergies, such as milk, wheat or peanuts, follow these simple tips:

• When making special food snacks, prepare the same item for the entire class. Avoid making special snacks for just one or two students.

• Serve cold water as one of the beverage choices at every party.

Teaching Kids to Cook

Teaching your kids to cook not only creates memories for all of you, but it also gives your children important lifetime skills. Since these valuable lessons are seldom taught in the classroom, your kitchen is the best place to turn your kid into a budding chef. Who knows, someday maybe you'll be dining in her newly opened restaurant! Learning to cook leads to learning other skills, such as menu planning, shopping and basic nutrition.

Getting started: Asking children what they want to learn to cook will give them control and lead to enthusiasm for helping in the kitchen. Naturally, they will choose things they like to eat, so learning to prepare French toast, dips, quesadillas, cookies and muffins will spark their interest. Working in the kitchen may be just the right incentive for your child to feel comfortable enough to try some new foods.

What to expect: Cooking requires learning many skills. Below you'll find a list based on ages that will help guide you to determine what your child can do in the kitchen. This list is very general. You know your child best, so make adjustments based on your child's abilities.

Ages 3 to 5: Children as young as 3 can help in the kitchen. Teach them to set the table; this helps them learn "left from right." They can also fold napkins, fill a bread basket, wash fruits and vegetables and tear lettuce. This is a good age to begin teaching kids how to measure ingredients.

Ages 6 to 8: Most children enjoy mixing cookie dough and dropping it onto cookie sheets or preparing cake or muffin batter. With help from an adult to read and explain recipes, kids can prepare simple recipes, such as sandwiches, salads, dips and no-bake desserts, at this age. They can begin to work at the range, stirring sauces, flipping pancakes and French toast, scrambling eggs and taking things out of the oven; kids may need to stand on a sturdy stool to safely work at the range. And a parent should be close by to avert any accidents.

Ages 9 to 12: Older kids can read recipes, measure ingredients, mix batters and handle more of the cooking themselves. They may still need help or advice from an adult when it comes to using the rangetop, oven, small appliances or sharp knives.

Ages 13 and older: By now, children who have had the opportunity to work with an adult in the kitchen should have the skills and confidence for independent cooking. Omelets, salads, quesadillas, chili, burgers, cookies and cakes are within their capabilities.

Safety in the kitchen: Parents should set ground rules and identify kitchen dangers. Explain the rules regarding kitchen appliances (rangetop, oven, microwave oven, blender, food processor, toaster, mixer, etc.) and sharp knives. Until your child has proven kitchen skills, the first rule should be that these items are off limits unless an adult is present in the kitchen to help. You'll need to set limits on when you feel your child is old enough to handle these items. Kids should be shown what to do in case of a spill, broken glass or a fire. Teach children the importance of washing their hands before and after handling food.

When they are ready, kids need to know how to safely handle hot things in the oven and on the range. (Hot mitts are a must.) Microwave ovens may seem a safe choice for kids, but foods can become very hot very quickly; certain containers are not safe to use in the microwave oven, resulting in fires or explosions. Before children use sharp knives they should be taught knife safety and have an opportunity to practice it with constant supervision. Toasters and blenders may seem straightforward to kids, but you will need to teach them how to avoid injury when using them.

Some things can be challenging for kids. For instance, you'll need to reach items on high shelves, handle large or heavy objects, and use tools meant for adult-sized hands. Mixing food by hand or with an electric stand mixer may be difficult for a child to do on the kitchen counter. The kitchen table may be just the right height.

Kitchen tools and appliances: Use your judgment to decide when your child is ready for new challenges, like rangetop cooking and using knives. When it comes to appliances and tools, most children can work in the kitchen as long as there is an adult present. Learning to use new appliances will happen over time—after one appliance is mastered, graduate to the next. For example, before using an electric hand mixer, a child should master the electric stand mixer. And before that he should learn to use the hand-held rotary beater.

Young children need to learn safe knife skills. Start them with a plastic knife or metal table knives before moving to sharp knives. Teach them to spread peanut butter and jelly first, then move on to slicing bananas, brownies and vegetables like celery and asparagus. Or you can cut zucchini and cucumbers in half lengthwise, then let your child cut crosswise slices. Show them how to place the food on a cutting board, hold it firmly and tuck their fingers out of the way. When they've mastered these skills, they can learn to cut round fruits and vegetables without them rolling and chop vegetables.

When your child begins to cook on the rangetop, pay extra attention. Turn handles of pans away from the edge of the range to avoid accidental spills. Make sure children use thick, dry potholders when handling hot pans. Keep toddlers and pets safely away from the work area.

Cooking can be educational: Kids feel very special when they are allowed to help out in the kitchen. In fact, cooking is a great educational tool for children. Working in the kitchen involves several valuable skills important to child development:

- Improving hand-eye coordination and reading skills.
- Planning a series of steps in a process.
- Using mathematical skills to measure ingredients and time the cooking of food.
- Reading and interpreting written instructions used in recipes.
- Expanding creative boundaries.
- Mastering team work when cooking with adults or other children.

Creating a cookbook: Children are proud of the recipes they prepare. Help them to collect their recipes in a cookbook of their own. Younger kids can assemble copies of their favorite recipes (older children can write or type them), take photos of the finished dish (or the family eating the food), and put them together in a notebook. Investing in a computer cookbook program for every family cook to use will teach computer and design skills as well.

fun food for kids

Veggie Pizza Cupcakes

1 can (12 ounces) refrigerated biscuits (10 biscuits)
1 teaspoon olive oil
1½ cups assorted diced fresh vegetables (red bell pepper, zucchini, summer squash, onion)
1½ cups RAGÚ® Organic Pasta Sauce or OLD WORLD STYLE® Pasta Sauce
½ cup shredded mozzarella cheese (about 2 ounces)

Preheat oven to 375°F. Unroll biscuits and press each into a 3-inch round. In 12-cup muffin pan, evenly press each biscuit into bottom and up side of each cup; chill until ready to fill.

In 10-inch skillet, heat olive oil over medium heat and cook vegetables, stirring occasionally, 5 minutes or until tender. Stir in Pasta Sauce and bring to a boil over high heat. Reduce heat to low and simmer 2 minutes or until slightly reduced.

Evenly spoon vegetable mixture into prepared muffin cups. Bake 15 minutes. Evenly sprinkle tops with cheese and bake an additional 5 minutes or until cheese is melted and biscuits are golden. Let stand 5 minutes. Gently remove pizza cups from muffin pan and serve.   *Makes 10 pizza cups*

Prep Time: 15 minutes
Cook Time: 20 minutes

Veggie Pizza Cupcakes

Mom's Tuna Casserole

2 cans (12 ounces each) tuna, drained and flaked
3 cups diced celery
3 cups crushed potato chips, divided
6 hard-cooked eggs, chopped
1 can (10¾ ounces) condensed cream of mushroom soup, undiluted
1 can (10¾ ounces) condensed cream of celery soup, undiluted
1 cup reduced-fat mayonnaise
1 teaspoon dried tarragon
1 teaspoon black pepper

Slow Cooker Directions

1. Combine tuna, celery, 2½ cups potato chips, eggs, soups, mayonnaise, tarragon and pepper in slow cooker; stir well.

2. Cover; cook on LOW 6 to 8 hours.

3. Sprinkle with remaining ½ cup potato chips.   *Makes 8 servings*

Dizzy Dogs

1 package (8 breadsticks) refrigerated breadstick dough
1 package (16 ounces) hot dogs (8 hot dogs)
1 egg white
  Sesame seeds and poppy seeds
  Mustard, ketchup and barbecue sauce (optional)

1. Preheat oven to 375°F.

2. Using 1 piece breadstick dough for each, wrap hot dogs with dough in spiral pattern. Brush breadstick dough with egg white and sprinkle with sesame seeds and poppy seeds. Place on ungreased baking sheet.

3. Bake 12 to 15 minutes or until light golden brown. Serve with condiments for dipping, if desired.   *Makes 8 servings*

Mom's Tuna Casserole

Spaghetti Sundaes

1 pound lean ground beef
½ cup Italian seasoned dry bread crumbs
1 egg
1 jar (26 ounces) RAGÚ® Organic Pasta Sauce
8 ounces spaghetti, cooked and drained

In medium bowl, combine ground beef, bread crumbs and egg; shape into 24 meatballs.

In 3-quart saucepan, bring Pasta Sauce to a boil over medium-high heat. Gently stir in uncooked meatballs.

Reduce heat to low and simmer covered, stirring occasionally, 20 minutes or until meatballs are done. Arrange spaghetti in 4 sundae dishes, then top each with 3 meatballs and sauce. Garnish, if desired, with parsley and grated Parmesan cheese. Serve remaining spaghetti, meatballs and Sauce on the side.

Makes 4 servings

Prep Time: 20 minutes
Cook Time: 20 minutes

tip

To determine when meatballs are done, cut one open. The meat should not be pink. You can also use an instant read thermometer to check doneness; meatballs should be cooked to 160°F.

Spaghetti Sundaes

Corn Dogs

8 hot dogs
8 wooden craft sticks
1 package (about 16 ounces) refrigerated grand-size corn biscuits
⅓ cup *French's*® Classic Yellow® Mustard
8 slices American cheese, cut in half

1. Preheat oven to 350°F. Insert 1 wooden craft stick halfway into each hot dog; set aside.

2. Separate biscuits. On floured board, press or roll each biscuit into a 7×4-inch oval. Spread *2 teaspoons* mustard lengthwise down center of each biscuit. Top each with 2 pieces of cheese. Place hot dog in center of biscuit. Fold top of dough over end of hot dog. Fold sides towards center enclosing hot dog. Pinch edges to seal.

3. Place corn dogs, seam side down, on greased baking sheet. Bake 20 to 25 minutes or until golden brown. Cool slightly before serving.   *Makes 8 servings*

Tip: Corn dogs may be made without wooden craft sticks.

Prep Time: 15 minutes
Cook Time: 20 minutes

Corn Dogs

Confetti Carnival Rice with Crunchy Chicken Nuggets

1 (4.9-ounce) package RICE-A-RONI® Chicken & Broccoli Flavor
1 tablespoon margarine or butter
  Crunchy Chicken Nuggets (recipe follows)
2 cups frozen or canned peas and corn, drained
½ cup pasteurized processed cheese, cut into ½-inch pieces

1. In large skillet over medium heat, sauté rice-pasta mix with margarine until pasta is golden brown. Slowly stir in 2 cups water and Special Seasonings; bring to a boil. Reduce heat to low. Cover; simmer 10 minutes. Meanwhile, prepare Crunchy Chicken Nuggets.

2. Stir in vegetables. Cover; simmer 5 to 7 minutes or until rice is tender. Stir in cheese. Let stand 3 minutes or until cheese is melted. Stir well before serving. Serve with Crunchy Chicken Nuggets or prepared frozen chicken nuggets.

Makes 4 servings

Prep Time: 20 minutes
Cook Time: 30 minutes

Crunchy Chicken Nuggets

3 cups potato chips, coarsely crushed
1 large egg
2 tablespoons milk
1 pound boneless, skinless chicken breasts, cut into 1½-inch chunks

1. Preheat oven to 450°F. Place crushed potato chips in medium bowl. Combine egg and milk with wire whisk in small bowl. Dip chicken in egg mixture, then coat with potato chips, pressing coating gently on each chicken piece.

2. Arrange chicken on lightly greased large baking sheet. Bake 12 minutes or until chicken is no longer pink inside.

Confetti Carnival Rice with Crunchy Chicken Nuggets

Sloppy Joe's Bun Buggy

 4 hot dog buns (not split)
16 thin slices cucumber or zucchini
24 matchstick-size carrot strips, 1 inch long
 4 ripe olives or pimiento-stuffed olives
   Nonstick cooking spray
 1 (10-ounce) package 93% lean ground turkey
1¼ cups pasta sauce
 ½ cup chopped broccoli stems
 2 teaspoons prepared mustard
 ½ teaspoon Worcestershire sauce
   Dash salt
   Dash black pepper
 4 small pretzel twists

1. Hollow out hot dog buns. Use toothpick to make four holes in sides of each bun to attach "wheels." Use toothpick to make one hole in center of each cucumber slice; push carrot strip through hole. Press into holes in buns, making "wheels" on buns.

2. Cut each olive in half horizontally. Use toothpick to make two holes in one end of each bun to attach "headlights." Use carrot strips to attach olives to buns, making "headlights."

3. Spray large nonstick skillet with cooking spray. Brown turkey in large skillet over medium-high heat, stirring to break up meat. Stir in pasta sauce, broccoli, mustard, Worcestershire sauce, salt and pepper. Cook, stirring occasionally until broccoli is tender.

4. Spoon turkey mixture into hollowed-out buns. Press pretzel twist into ground turkey mixture, making "windshield" on each buggy.   *Makes 4 servings*

Sloppy Joe's Bun Buggy

Silly Face Pizza

1 (10 ounce) prebaked pizza crust
1 cup RAGÚ® OLD WORLD STYLE® Pasta Sauce
1½ cups shredded mozzarella cheese (about 6 ounces)
Silly Face Garnishes*

*For Silly Face Garnishes, use ½ cup cooked rotini pasta for hair, broccoli florets for eyebrows, roasted red peppers and peas for eyes, baby carrot half for nose and pepperoni slice for mouth.

Preheat oven to 450°F.

On baking sheet, place pizza crust. Evenly top with Pasta Sauce, then cheese and Silly Face Garnishes. Bake 12 minutes or until cheese is melted and crust is golden.

Makes 4 servings

Prep Time: 20 minutes
Cook Time: 12 minutes

Kiddy Quesadillas

1 can (15 ounces) VEG•ALL® Original Mixed Vegetables, drained
1 pound ground beef, cooked and drained
2 cups shredded taco cheese
½ cup mild salsa
Salt & pepper to taste
10 teaspoons vegetable oil
10 (6-inch) flour tortillas

Combine the first 5 ingredients in a medium size bowl.

Heat 1 teaspoon of oil in a 10 or 12-inch nonstick skillet over medium heat. Spread ½ cup of beef mixture onto 1 tortilla. Carefully transfer to hot skillet.

Cook for 1½ to 2 minutes or until golden brown. Fold over one side with a spatula. Cook an additional 30 to 45 seconds.

Remove from skillet, cut in half and serve. Repeat with remaining filling and tortillas if desired or refrigerate until needed.

Makes 10 quesadillas

Silly Face Pizza

Zippity Hot Doggity Tacos

1 small onion, finely chopped
**1 tablespoon *Frank's® RedHot®* Original Cayenne Pepper Sauce or
   French's® Worcestershire Sauce**
4 frankfurters, chopped
1 can (10½ ounces) red kidney or black beans, drained
1 can (8 ounces) tomato sauce
1 teaspoon chili powder
8 taco shells, heated
1 cup *French's®* French Fried Onions
   **Garnish: chopped tomatoes, shredded lettuce, sliced olives, sour
   cream, shredded cheese**

1. Heat *1 tablespoon oil* in 12-inch nonstick skillet over medium-high heat. Cook onion, 3 minutes or until crisp-tender. Stir in remaining ingredients except taco shells, French Fried Onions and garnishes. Bring to boiling. Reduce heat to medium-low and cook 5 minutes, stirring occasionally.

2. To serve, spoon chili into taco shells. Garnish as desired and sprinkle with French Fried Onions. Splash on **Frank's RedHot** Sauce for extra zip!   *Makes 4 servings*

Prep Time: 5 minutes
Cook Time: 8 minutes

tip

Cooked dried beans like the red kidney beans in this recipe are a good source of protein and a great source of fiber—plus they are extremely low in fat.

Zippity Hot Doggity Tacos

Barbecue Flying Saucers with Vegetable Martians

½ teaspoon black pepper*
1 (10-ounce) pork tenderloin*
¼ cup barbecue sauce
½ teaspoon prepared mustard
1 (7½-ounce) package (10) refrigerated buttermilk biscuits
1 egg yolk (optional)
3 to 4 drops food coloring (optional)
Vegetable Martians (recipe follows)

*Substitute 10 ounces lean deli roasted pork for pork tenderloin and pepper, if desired.

1. Preheat oven to 425°F. Rub pepper on pork tenderloin. Place pork in shallow roasting pan. Roast 15 to 25 minutes or until meat thermometer inserted into thickest part of meat registers 160°F. Remove from oven; let stand 5 minutes. Shred pork.

2. *Reduce oven temperature to 400°F.* Stir together barbecue sauce and mustard. Toss with shredded pork.

3. Roll each biscuit on lightly floured surface into 4-inch circle. Place one fifth of pork mixture on each of five circles. Moisten edges. Top with remaining biscuit circles. Crimp edges to seal.

4. Stir together egg yolk, 1 teaspoon water and food coloring to make egg-wash paint, if desired. Using clean paintbrush, paint designs on "flying saucers." Place on baking sheet. Bake 11 to 13 minutes or until golden.   *Makes 5 servings*

Vegetable Martians

10 cherry tomatoes, baby pattypan squash or combination
5 to 10 thin slices cucumber or zucchini
¼ teaspoon reduced-fat soft cream cheese or mustard
10 currants
10 chow mein noodles

Skewer vegetables on toothpicks to form Martian bodies. Use cream cheese for mouths and to attach currants for eyes. Press 2 chow mein noodles into top of each Martian for antennae. Remove toothpicks before serving.   *Makes 5 Martians*

Barbecue Flying Saucer with Vegetable Martian

Salsa Macaroni & Cheese

1 jar (16 ounces) RAGÚ® Cheese Creations!® Double Cheddar Sauce
1 cup prepared mild salsa
8 ounces elbow macaroni, cooked and drained

1. In 2-quart saucepan, heat Ragú Cheese Creations! Sauce over medium heat. Stir in salsa; heat through.

2. Toss with hot macaroni. Serve immediately.   *Makes 4 servings*

Prep Time: 5 minutes
Cook Time: 15 minutes

Crunchy Turkey Pita Pockets

1 cup diced cooked turkey or chicken breast or
**   reduced-sodium deli turkey breast**
½ cup packaged coleslaw mix
½ cup dried cranberries
¼ cup shredded carrots
2 tablespoons reduced-fat mayonnaise
1 tablespoon honey mustard
2 (6-inch) whole wheat pita bread rounds

1. Combine turkey, coleslaw mix, cranberries, carrots, mayonnaise and mustard in small bowl; mix well.

2. Cut pita rounds in half; fill with turkey mixture. Garnish as desired.

Makes 2 servings

Salsa Macaroni & Cheese

Little Piggy Pies

2 cups frozen mixed vegetables (carrots, potatoes, peas, celery, green beans, corn, onions and/or lima beans)
1 can (10¾ ounces) reduced-fat condensed cream of chicken soup, undiluted
8 ounces chopped cooked chicken
⅓ cup plain low-fat yogurt
⅓ cup water
½ teaspoon dried thyme
¼ teaspoon poultry seasoning or ground sage
⅛ teaspoon garlic powder
1 package (10 biscuits) refrigerated buttermilk biscuits

1. Preheat oven to 400°F.

2. Remove 10 green peas from frozen mixed vegetables; set aside. Combine remaining vegetables, soup, chicken, yogurt, water, thyme, poultry seasoning and garlic powder in medium saucepan. Bring to a boil, stirring frequently. Cover; keep warm.

3. Press five biscuits into 3-inch circles. Cut each remaining biscuit into eight wedges. Place two wedges on top of each circle; fold points down to form ears. Roll one wedge into small ball; place in center of each circle to form pig's snout. Use tip of spoon handle to make indents in snout for nostrils. Place 2 reserved green peas on each circle for eyes.

4. Spoon hot chicken mixture into 5 (10-ounce) custard cups. Place one biscuit "pig" on top of each. Place remaining biscuit wedges around each "pig" on top of chicken mixture, twisting one wedge "tail" for each. Bake 9 to 11 minutes or until biscuits are golden. *Makes 5 servings*

Prep Time: 10 minutes
Bake Time: 11 minutes

Little Piggy Pie

Chicken Rolls

2 teaspoons vegetable oil
1 package (10 ounces) frozen stir-fry vegetables
2 packages (8 ounces) cooked diced chicken
1 tablespoon hot Asian chili sauce with garlic (optional)
1 tablespoon hoisin sauce
1 package (15½ ounces) refrigerated large crescent rolls
All-purpose flour
3 tablespoons orange marmalade
1 tablespoon plus 1 teaspoon white wine vinegar
1 tablespoon plus 1 teaspoon soy sauce

1. Preheat oven to 350°F.

2. Heat oil in large skillet. Add frozen vegetables; cook until liquid has evaporated, stirring frequently. Add chicken, chili sauce, if desired, and hoisin sauce. Stir; remove from heat. Cool 5 minutes.

3. Separate crescent rolls on lightly floured board. Place ½ cup chicken filling on wide end of each roll; roll up to narrow point. Place rolls, seam side down, on ungreased baking sheet. Bake 18 to 20 minutes or until golden.

4. Combine orange marmalade, vinegar and soy sauce. Serve with Chicken Rolls.

Makes 6 servings

Chicken Roll

Octo-Dogs and Shells

4 refrigerated low-fat hot dogs
1½ cups uncooked small shell pasta
1½ cups frozen mixed vegetables
1 cup prepared Alfredo sauce
Prepared yellow mustard in squeeze bottle
Cheese-flavored fish-shaped crackers

1. Lay 1 hot dog on cutting surface. Starting 1 inch from one end of hot dog, slice hot dog lengthwise in half. Roll hot dog ¼ turn. Starting 1 inch from same end, slice in half lengthwise again, making 4 segments connected at top. Slice each segment in half lengthwise, creating a total of 8 "legs." Repeat with remaining hot dogs.

2. Place hot dogs in medium saucepan; cover with water. Bring to a boil over medium-high heat. Remove from heat; set aside.

3. Meanwhile, cook pasta according to package directions, stirring in vegetables during last 3 minutes of cooking time. Drain; return to pan. Stir in Alfredo sauce. Heat over low heat until heated through. Divide pasta mixture between 4 plates.

4. Drain octo-dogs. Arrange one octo-dog on top of pasta mixture on each plate. Draw faces on "heads" of octo-dogs with mustard. Sprinkle crackers over pasta.

Makes 4 servings

Octo-Dog and Shells

Kid's Choice Meatballs

1½ pounds ground beef
¼ cup dry seasoned bread crumbs
¼ cup grated Parmesan cheese
3 tablespoons *French's*® Worcestershire Sauce
1 egg
2 jars (14 ounces each) spaghetti sauce

1. Preheat oven to 425°F. In bowl, gently mix beef, bread crumbs, cheese, Worcestershire and egg. Shape into 1-inch meatballs. Place on rack in roasting pan. Bake 15 minutes or until cooked through (160°F).

2. In large saucepan, combine meatballs and spaghetti sauce. Cook until heated through. Serve over cooked pasta.   *Makes 6 to 8 servings (about 48 meatballs)*

Prep Time: 10 minutes
Cook Time: 20 minutes

tip

On waxed paper, pat meat mixture into 8×6×1-inch rectangle. With knife, cut crosswise and lengthwise into 1-inch-wide rows. Roll each small square into a ball.

Kid's Choice Meatballs

Hot Diggity Dots & Twisters

⅔ cup milk
2 tablespoons margarine or butter
1 (4.8-ounce) package PASTA RONI® Four Cheese Flavor with
    Corkscrew Pasta
1½ cups frozen peas
4 hot dogs, cut into ½-inch pieces
2 teaspoons mustard

1. In large saucepan, bring 1¼ cups water, milk and margarine just to a boil.

2. Stir in pasta, peas and Special Seasonings; return to a boil. Reduce heat to medium. Gently boil, uncovered, 7 to 8 minutes or until pasta is tender, stirring occasionally.

3. Stir in hot dogs and mustard. Let stand 3 to 5 minutes before serving.

Makes 4 servings

Prep Time: 5 minutes
Cook Time: 15 minutes

tip

Recipes with cute or wacky names are sometimes all it takes to catch kids' attention and get them to try a new dish.

Hot Diggity Dots & Twisters

easy family meals

Spicy Chicken Stromboli

1 cup frozen broccoli florets, thawed
1 can (10 ounces) diced chicken
1½ cups (6 ounces) shredded Monterey Jack cheese with jalapeño peppers
¼ cup chunky salsa
2 green onions, chopped
1 package (10 ounces) refrigerated pizza dough

1. Preheat oven to 400°F. Coarsely chop broccoli. Combine broccoli, chicken, cheese, salsa and green onions in small bowl.

2. Unroll pizza dough. Pat into 15×10-inch rectangle. Sprinkle broccoli mixture evenly over top. Starting with long side, tightly roll into log jelly-roll style. Pinch seam to seal. Place on baking sheet, seam side down.

3. Bake 15 to 20 minutes or until golden brown. Transfer to wire rack to cool slightly. Slice and serve warm. *Makes 6 servings*

Serving Suggestion: Serve with salsa on the side for dipping or pour salsa on top of slices for a boost of added flavor.

Note: You may substitute plain Monterey Jack cheese or Cheddar cheese for the the Monterey Jack with jalapeño peppers.

Prep and Cook Time: 30 minutes

Spicy Chicken Stromboli

Backyard Barbecue Burgers

1½ pounds ground beef
⅓ cup barbecue sauce, divided
1 to 2 tomatoes, cut into slices
1 onion, cut into slices
1 to 2 tablespoons olive oil
6 kaiser rolls, split
Green or red leaf lettuce

1. Prepare grill for direct grilling. Combine ground beef and 2 tablespoons barbecue sauce in large bowl. Shape into six 1-inch-thick patties.

2. Place patties on grid. Grill, covered, 8 to 10 minutes over medium coals (or, uncovered, 13 to 15 minutes) or until 160°F in centers of patties, turning and brushing often with remaining barbecue sauce.

3. Meanwhile, brush tomato and onion slices* with oil. Place on grid. Grill tomato slices 2 to 3 minutes and onion slices about 10 minutes.

4. Just before serving, place rolls, cut side down, on grid; grill until lightly toasted. Serve patties on rolls with tomatoes, onions and lettuce.   *Makes 6 servings*

Onion slices may be cooked in 1 tablespoon oil in large skillet over medium heat 10 minutes until tender and slightly brown.

Backyard Barbecue Burger

Taco Two-Zies

1 pound ground beef
2 packages (1 ounce each) LAWRY'S® Taco Spices & Seasonings
⅔ cup water
1 can (1 pound 14 ounces) refried beans, warmed
10 small flour tortillas (fajita size), warmed to soften
10 jumbo size taco shells, heated according to package directions

Taco Toppings
Shredded lettuce, shredded Cheddar cheese and chopped tomatoes

In large skillet, brown ground beef over medium-high heat until crumbly; drain fat. Stir in 1 package Taco Spices & Seasonings and water. Bring to a boil; reduce heat to low and cook, uncovered, 10 minutes, stirring occasionally. In medium bowl, mix together beans and remaining package Taco Spices & Seasonings. Spread about ⅓-cup seasoned beans all the way to edge of each flour tortilla. Place a taco shell on center of each bean-tortilla and fold edges up around shell, lightly pressing to 'stick' tortilla to shell. Fill each taco with about 3 tablespoons taco meat. Top with your choice of taco toppings.   *Makes 10 tacos*

Variations: You may use lean ground turkey, chicken or pork in place of the ground beef. LAWRY'S® Chicken Taco Spices & Seasonings or Lawry's® Hot Taco Spices & Seasonings may be substituted for the Taco Spices & Seasonings.

Prep Time: 8 to 10 minutes
Cook Time: 15 minutes

Taco Two-Zies

Oven-Baked Chicken Parmesan

4 boneless, skinless chicken breast halves (about 1¼ pounds)
1 egg, lightly beaten
¾ cup Italian seasoned dry bread crumbs
1 jar (26 ounces) RAGÚ® Old World Style® Pasta Sauce
1 cup shredded mozzarella cheese (about 4 ounces)

1. Preheat oven to 400°F. Dip chicken in egg, then bread crumbs, coating well.

2. In 13×9-inch glass baking dish, arrange chicken. Bake uncovered 20 minutes.

3. Pour Ragú Pasta Sauce over chicken, then top with cheese. Bake an additional 10 minutes or until chicken is no longer pink in center. Serve, if desired, with hot cooked pasta. *Makes 4 servings*

Prep Time: 10 minutes
Cook Time: 30 minutes

Quick Taco Macaroni & Cheese

1 package (12 ounces) large elbow macaroni (4 cups dried pasta)
1 tablespoon LAWRY'S® Seasoned Salt
1 pound lean ground beef or turkey
1 package (1 ounce) LAWRY'S® Taco Spices & Seasonings
2 cups (8 ounces) shredded Colby longhorn cheese
2 cups (8 ounces) shredded mild cheddar cheese
2 cups milk
3 eggs, beaten

In large stockpot, boil macaroni in unsalted water just until tender. Drain and toss with Seasoned Salt. Meanwhile in medium skillet, brown ground meat; drain fat. Stir in Taco Spices & Seasonings. Spray 13×9×2-inch baking dish with nonstick cooking spray. Layer half of macaroni in bottom of dish. Top with half of cheeses. Spread taco meat over top and repeat layers of macaroni and cheeses. In medium bowl, beat together milk and eggs. Pour egg mixture over top of casserole. Bake in preheated 350°F oven for 30 to 35 minutes, until golden brown. *Makes 6 to 8 servings*

Prep Time: 20 to 22 minutes
Cook Time: 30 to 35 minutes

Oven-Baked Chicken Parmesan

Round Steak

1 boneless beef round steak (1½ pounds), trimmed and cut into 4 pieces
¼ cup all-purpose flour
1 teaspoon black pepper
½ teaspoon salt
1 tablespoon vegetable oil
1 can (10¾ ounces) condensed cream of mushroom soup, undiluted
¾ cup water
1 medium onion, quartered
1 can (4 ounces) sliced mushrooms, drained
¼ cup milk
1 package (1 ounce) dry onion soup mix
1 bay leaf
Salt
Black pepper
Ground sage
Dried thyme

Slow Cooker Directions

1. Place steaks in large resealable food storage bag. Close bag and pound with meat mallet to tenderize steaks.

2. Combine flour, 1 teaspoon pepper and ½ teaspoon salt in small bowl; add to bag with steaks. Shake to coat meat evenly.

3. Heat oil in large nonstick skillet. Remove steaks from bag; shake off excess flour. Add steaks to skillet; brown both sides. Transfer steaks and pan juices to slow cooker.

4. Add canned soup, water, onion, mushrooms, milk, dry soup mix and bay leaf to slow cooker. Season with salt, pepper, sage and thyme; mix well.

5. Cover; cook on LOW 5 to 6 hours or until steaks are tender. Remove and discard bay leaf before serving. *Makes 4 servings*

Round Steak

Ranch Crispy Chicken

¼ cup unseasoned dry bread crumbs or cornflake crumbs
1 packet (1 ounce) HIDDEN VALLEY® The Original Ranch® Salad
    Dressing & Seasoning Mix
6 bone-in chicken pieces

Combine bread crumbs and salad dressing & seasoning mix in a gallon-size Glad® Zipper Storage Bag. Add chicken pieces; seal bag. Shake to coat chicken. Bake chicken on ungreased baking pan at 375°F for 50 minutes or until no longer pink in center and juices run clear. *Makes 4 to 6 servings*

School Night Chicken Rice Taco Toss

1 (6.9-ounce) package RICE-A-RONI® Chicken Flavor
2 tablespoons margarine or butter
1 (16-ounce) jar salsa
1 pound boneless, skinless chicken breasts, chopped
1 cup frozen or canned corn, drained
4 cups shredded lettuce
½ cup (2 ounces) shredded Cheddar cheese
2 cups tortilla chips, coarsely broken
1 medium tomato, chopped

1. In large skillet over medium-high heat, sauté rice-vermicelli mix with margarine until vermicelli is golden brown.

2. Slowly stir in 2 cups water, salsa, chicken and Special Seasonings. Bring to a boil. Reduce heat to low. Cover; simmer 10 minutes.

3. Stir in corn. Cover; simmer 5 to 10 minutes or until rice is tender and chicken is no longer pink inside.

4. Arrange lettuce on large serving platter. Top with chicken-rice mixture. Sprinkle with cheese and tortilla chips. Garnish with tomato. *Makes 6 servings*

Prep Time: 10 minutes
Cook Time: 30 minutes

Ranch Crispy Chicken

Italian Sloppy Joes

1 pound hot or mild bulk Italian sausage (or sausage links with casings removed)
1 small onion, chopped
1 small green or yellow bell pepper, chopped
1 cup prepared spaghetti sauce
1 teaspoon dried basil leaves
4 Kaiser rolls, split, toasted
4 slices SARGENTO® Deli Style Sliced Mozzarella Cheese

1. Cook sausage with onion and bell pepper in a large skillet until no longer pink, stirring often; drain.

2. Add spaghetti sauce and basil; simmer 5 to 7 minutes or until thickened, stirring occasionally.

3. Fill each roll with sausage mixture and a slice of cheese.   *Makes 4 servings*

Prep time: 8 minutes
Cook time: 12 minutes

Ranch Bacon and Egg Salad Sandwich

6 hard-cooked eggs, cooled and peeled
¼ cup HIDDEN VALLEY® The Original Ranch® Dressing
¼ cup diced celery
3 tablespoons crisp-cooked, crumbled bacon*
1 tablespoon diced green onion
8 slices sandwich bread
Lettuce and tomato (optional)

*Bacon pieces can be used.

Coarsely chop eggs. Combine with dressing, celery, bacon and onion in a medium mixing bowl; mix well. Chill until just before serving. Spread salad evenly on 4 bread slices; arrange lettuce and tomato on egg salad, if desired. Top with remaining bread slices.   *Makes 4 sandwiches (about 2 cups salad)*

Italian Sloppy Joe

Chicken Normandy Style

2 tablespoons butter, divided
3 cups peeled, thinly sliced apples, such as Fuji or Braeburn (about 3 apples)
1 pound ground chicken
¼ cup apple juice
1 can (10¾ ounces) condensed cream of chicken soup, undiluted
¼ cup finely chopped green onions
2 teaspoons fresh minced sage *or* ½ teaspoon dried sage
¼ teaspoon black pepper
1 package (12 ounces) egg noodles, cooked and drained

1. Preheat oven to 350°F. Grease 9-inch square casserole dish.

2. Melt 1 tablespoon butter in 12-inch nonstick skillet. Add apple slices; cook and stir over medium heat 7 to 10 minutes or until tender. Remove apple slices from skillet.

3. In same skillet, brown chicken over medium heat, stirring to break up meat. Stir in juice; cook 2 minutes. Stir in soup, green onions, sage, pepper and apple slices. Simmer 5 minutes.

4. Toss noodles with remaining 1 tablespoon butter. Spoon into prepared casserole. Top with chicken mixture. Bake 15 minutes or until hot.   *Makes 4 servings*

Note: Ground turkey, ground pork or tofu crumbles can be substituted for chicken, if desired.

Chicken Normandy Style

Easy Make-at-Home Chinese Chicken

3 tablespoons frozen orange juice concentrate, thawed
2 tablespoons reduced-sodium soy sauce
2 tablespoons water
¾ teaspoon cornstarch
¼ teaspoon garlic powder
  Nonstick cooking spray
2 carrots, sliced
1 package (12 ounces) broccoli and cauliflower florets
2 teaspoons canola oil
¾ pound boneless skinless chicken breasts, cut into bite-size pieces
  Hot cooked rice

1. For sauce, stir together juice concentrate, soy sauce, water, cornstarch and garlic powder until smooth; set aside.

2. Spray nonstick wok or large skillet with cooking spray. Heat over high heat. Stir-fry carrots 1 minute. Add broccoli and cauliflower to wok. Stir-fry 2 to 3 minutes or until vegetables are crisp-tender. Remove vegetables from wok; set aside.

3. Add oil to wok. Stir-fry chicken 2 to 3 minutes or until no longer pink. Push chicken up side of wok. Stir sauce mixture; pour into wok. Bring sauce to a boil, stirring constantly. Return vegetables to wok; stir chicken into sauce mixture. Cook and stir until mixture is heated through. Serve with hot cooked rice.   *Makes 4 servings*

tip

For a fun look, make carrot slices in the shape of flowers. Using a clean bottle opener or vegetable stripper, make 4 to 5 lengthwise cuts along each carrot. Cut carrots crosswise into slices.

Easy Make-at-Home Chinese Chicken

Sweet & Saucy Ribs

2 pounds pork baby back ribs
1 teaspoon black pepper
2½ cups barbecue sauce (not mesquite flavored)
1 jar (8 ounces) cherry jam or preserves
1 tablespoon Dijon mustard
¼ teaspoon salt
Additional salt and black pepper (optional)

Slow Cooker Directions

1. Trim excess fat from ribs. Rub 1 teaspoon pepper over ribs. Cut ribs into 2-rib portions; place in slow cooker.

2. Combine barbecue sauce, jam, mustard and ¼ teaspoon salt in small bowl; pour over ribs.

3. Cover; cook on LOW 6 to 8 hours or until ribs are tender. Season with additional salt and pepper, if desired. Serve ribs with sauce. *Makes 4 servings*

Prep Time: 10 minutes
Cook Time: 6 to 8 hours (LOW) • 3 to 4 hours (HIGH)

Sweet & Saucy Ribs

Mini Chicken Pot Pies

1 container (about 16 ounces) refrigerated reduced-fat buttermilk biscuits
1½ cups milk
1 package (1.8 ounces) white sauce mix
2 cups cut-up cooked chicken
1 cup frozen assorted vegetables, partially thawed
2 cups shredded Cheddar cheese
2 cups *French's*® French Fried Onions

1. Preheat oven to 400°F. Separate biscuits; press into 8 (8-ounce) custard cups, pressing up sides to form crust.

2. Whisk milk and sauce mix in medium saucepan. Bring to boiling over medium-high heat. Reduce heat to medium-low; simmer 1 minute, whisking constantly, until thickened. Stir in chicken and vegetables.

3. Spoon about ⅓ cup chicken mixture into each crust. Place cups on baking sheet. Bake 15 minutes or until golden brown. Top each with cheese and French Fried Onions. Bake 3 minutes or until golden. To serve, remove from cups and transfer to serving plates. *Makes 8 servings*

Prep Time: 15 minutes
Cook Time: about 20 minutes

Mini Chicken Pot Pies

Hungarian Goulash Casserole

 1 pound ground pork
¼ teaspoon salt
¼ teaspoon ground nutmeg
¼ teaspoon black pepper
 1 tablespoon vegetable oil
 1 cup reduced-fat sour cream, divided
 1 tablespoon cornstarch
 1 can (10¾ ounces) cream of celery soup, undiluted
 1 cup milk
 1 teaspoon sweet Hungarian paprika
 1 package (12 ounces) egg noodles, cooked and drained
 2 teaspoons minced fresh dill (optional)

1. Preheat oven to 325°F. Spray 3-quart casserole dish with nonstick cooking spray; set aside.

2. Combine pork, salt, nutmeg and pepper in medium bowl. Shape into 1-inch meatballs. Heat oil in large skillet over medium-high heat. Add meatballs. Cook 10 minutes or until browned on all sides and no longer pink in center. Remove meatballs from skillet; discard drippings.

3. Stir together ¼ cup sour cream and cornstarch in small bowl until smooth. Add remaining ¾ cup sour cream, soup, milk, cornstarch mixture and paprika to skillet. Stir until well blended.

4. Spoon noodles into prepared dish. Arrange meatballs over noodles and cover with sauce. Bake 20 minutes or until hot. Sprinkle with dill, if desired.

Make 4 to 6 servings

Hungarian Goulash Casserole

Slow Cooker Pepper Steak

2 tablespoons vegetable oil
3 pounds boneless beef top sirloin steak, cut into strips
1 tablespoon minced garlic (5 to 6 cloves)
1 medium onion, chopped
½ cup reduced-sodium soy sauce
2 teaspoons sugar
1 teaspoon salt
½ teaspoon ground ginger
½ teaspoon black pepper
3 green bell peppers, cut into strips
¼ cup cold water
1 tablespoon cornstarch
Hot cooked rice

Slow Cooker Directions

1. Heat oil in large skillet over medium heat. Brown steak strips in two batches. Add garlic; cook and stir 2 minutes. Transfer meat, garlic and pan juices to slow cooker.

2. Add onion, soy sauce, sugar, salt, ginger and black pepper to slow cooker; mix well. Cover; cook on LOW 6 to 8 hours or until meat is tender (up to 10 hours).

3. Add bell pepper during last hour of cooking. Blend water and cornstarch until smooth; stir into slow cooker. Cook, uncovered, on HIGH 15 minutes or until thickened. Serve with rice. *Makes 6 to 8 servings*

tip

You can substitute brown rice in this recipe. The nutty flavor of the brown rice blends well with Asian foods like this Pepper Steak.

Slow Cooker Pepper Steak

Chicken and Stuffing

½ cup all-purpose flour
¾ teaspoon seasoned salt
¾ teaspoon black pepper
4 to 6 boneless skinless chicken breasts (about 1 to 1½ pounds)
¼ cup (½ stick) butter
2 cans (10¾ ounces each) condensed cream of mushroom soup, undiluted
1 package (12 ounces) seasoned stuffing mix, plus ingredients to prepare mix

Slow Cooker Directions

1. Combine flour, seasoned salt and pepper in large resealable food storage bag. Add chicken; shake to coat with flour mixture.

2. Melt butter in large skillet over medium-low heat. Brown chicken on both sides. Place in slow cooker; pour soup over chicken.

3. Prepare stuffing according to package directions, decreasing liquid by half. Arrange stuffing over chicken. Cover; cook on HIGH 3 to 4 hours.

Makes 4 to 6 servings

tip

It may not seem like there's enough liquid in this recipe after assembling ingredients. However, as food heats in a slow cooker, the steam condenses to liquid that accumulates and dilutes the ingredients. The end result is a perfectly prepared meal.

Chicken and Stuffing

Tamale Pies

1 pound ground pork, beef or turkey
1 tablespoon chili powder
2 cloves garlic, minced
½ teaspoon salt
1 cup (4 ounces) shredded Monterey-Jack cheese
1 package (8½ ounces) corn bread mix, plus ingredients to prepare mix
1 can (11 ounces) Mexican-style corn, drained
6 sheets (12×12 inches) heavy-duty foil, lightly sprayed with nonstick cooking spray
¾ cup mild or hot salsa
¼ cup regular or fat-free sour cream
6 cilantro sprigs (optional)

1. Preheat oven to 450°F.

2. Combine pork, chili powder, garlic and salt in nonstick skillet. Cook over medium-high heat, stirring to break up meat, until pork is no longer pink and moisture has evaporated. Remove from heat; stir in cheese. Set aside.

3. Prepare corn bread mix according to package directions. Stir in corn.

4. Place about ½ cup pork mixture in center of one foil sheet; flatten slightly. Top with ¼ cup corn bread mix. Spread lightly over pork. (It is not necessary to cover sides of pork.) Double fold sides and ends of foil to seal packet, leaving head space for heat circulation. Repeat with remaining pork mixture, corn bread mix and foil to make 5 more packets. Place packets on baking sheet.

5. Bake 12 minutes. Let stand 5 minutes. Carefully open packets and transfer contents to serving plates. Serve with salsa, sour cream and cilantro sprigs, if desired.

Makes 6 servings

Tamale Pie

Snappy Citrus Salad with Turkey

½ pound fresh sugar snap or snow peas
10 slices deli mesquite or smoked turkey breast
3 to 4 Texas Red Grapefruit, peeled and sectioned
Boston lettuce leaves
1 pint fresh strawberries
Strawberry Poppy Seed Vinaigrette (recipe follows)

Snap off stem ends of sugar snap peas. Plunge peas into boiling water for 1 minute, drain, then plunge into ice water. Drain and pat dry. Roll up turkey slices and cut crosswise into halves.

On each of 4 dinner plates, first arrange 2 peas, so ends are about 1-inch from rim of plate. About halfway from center of each plate, place 2 grapefruit sections and 1 turkey roll next to sugar snaps, and continue alternating peas, grapefruit and turkey. In center of each plate, place 1 or 2 small lettuce leaves. Wash berries and cut into halves; arrange about 6 to 8 strawberry halves over lettuce. Serve immediately with Strawberry Poppy Seed Vinaigrette. *Makes 4 servings*

Strawberry Poppy Seed Vinaigrette

2 tablespoons strawberry vinegar
1 tablespoon sugar
1 tablespoon chopped onion
¼ teaspoon salt
¼ cup salad oil
1 teaspoon poppy seeds

Combine vinegar, sugar, onion and salt in blender; process until smooth. Add oil and process until thickened. Stir in poppy seeds. *Makes ½ cup or about 4 servings*

Favorite recipe from **TexaSweet Citrus Marketing, Inc.**

Snappy Citrus Salad with Turkey

Slow Cooker Steak Fajitas

1 beef flank steak (about 1 pound)
1 medium onion, cut into strips
½ cup medium salsa
2 tablespoons fresh lime juice
2 tablespoons chopped fresh cilantro
2 cloves garlic, minced
1 tablespoon chili powder
1 teaspoon ground cumin
½ teaspoon salt
1 small green bell pepper, cut into strips
1 small red bell pepper, cut into strips
Flour tortillas, warmed
Additional salsa

Slow Cooker Directions

1. Cut flank steak lengthwise in half, then crosswise into thin strips. Combine onion, ½ cup salsa, lime juice, cilantro, garlic, chili powder, cumin and salt in slow cooker.

2. Cover; cook on LOW 5 to 6 hours. Add bell peppers. Cover; cook on LOW 1 hour.

3. Serve with flour tortillas and additional salsa. *Makes 4 servings*

Prep Time: 20 minutes
Cook Time: 6 to 7 hours

Slow Cooker Steak Fajitas

By-the-Sea Casserole

1 bag (16 ounces) BIRDS EYE® frozen Mixed Vegetables
2 cans (6 ounces each) tuna in water, drained
1 can (10¾ ounces) cream of celery soup, undiluted
1 cup uncooked instant rice
1 cup 1% milk
1 cup cheese-flavored fish-shaped crackers

- In medium bowl, combine vegetables and tuna.

- Stir in soup, rice and milk.

- Place tuna mixture in 1½-quart microwave-safe casserole dish; cover and microwave on HIGH 6 minutes. Stir; microwave, covered, 6 to 8 minutes more or until rice is tender.

- Stir casserole and sprinkle with crackers. *Makes 6 servings*

Prep Time: 10 minutes
Cook Time: 15 minutes

Golden Chicken Nuggets

1 envelope LIPTON® RECIPE SECRETS® Golden Onion Soup Mix
½ cup plain dry bread crumbs
1½ pounds boneless, skinless chicken breasts, cut into 2-inch pieces
2 tablespoons margarine or butter, melted

1. Preheat oven to 425°F. In small bowl, combine soup mix and bread crumbs. Dip chicken in bread crumb mixture until evenly coated.

2. On lightly greased cookie sheet, arrange chicken; drizzle with margarine.

3. Bake uncovered 15 minutes or until chicken is no longer pink in center, turning once. *Makes 6 servings*

Tip: Also terrific with Lipton® Recipe Secrets® Onion, Onion-Mushroom or Savory Herb with Garlic Soup Mix.

Prep Time: 10 minutes
Cook Time: 15 minutes

By-the-Sea Casserole

Hidden Valley® Chopstick Chicken Salad

1 packet (1 ounce) HIDDEN VALLEY® The Original Ranch® Salad Dressing & Seasoning Mix
1 cup milk
1 cup mayonnaise
2 tablespoons soy sauce
8 cups torn lettuce
2 cups cubed or shredded cooked chicken
1 cup chopped green onions
1 cup chopped water chestnuts
1 cup toasted sliced almonds (optional)

In a bowl, combine salad dressing & seasoning mix with milk and mayonnaise. Mix well. Cover and refrigerate. Chill 30 minutes to thicken. Stir in soy sauce. Toss with lettuce, chicken, onions and water chestnuts; top with almonds, if desired.

Makes 4 to 6 servings

Note: To make Lower Fat Hidden Valley® The Original Ranch® Salad Dressing & Seasoning Mix, substitute low-fat milk and light mayonnaise for regular milk and mayonnaise.

tip

If you don't have leftover chicken, look for precooked chicken strips in the meat case or purchase a rotisserie chicken and cut it up. For 2 cups cooked chicken, roast or poach 12 ounces of boneless skinless chicken breast.

Hidden Valley® Chopstick Chicken Salad

Mexi-Tortilla Casserole

1 tablespoon vegetable oil
1 small onion, chopped
1 pound ground pork
1 can (14½ ounces) diced tomatoes, undrained
1 teaspoon dried oregano
¼ teaspoon salt
¼ teaspoon ground cumin
¼ teaspoon black pepper
1½ cups (6 ounces) shredded pepper-Jack or taco-flavored cheese
2 cups tortilla chips
½ cup reduced-fat sour cream
1 can (4 ounces) diced green chilies, drained
2 tablespoons minced cilantro

1. Preheat oven to 350°F.

2. Heat oil in large skillet over medium heat. Cook and stir onion 5 minutes or until tender. Brown pork, stirring to separate meat. Drain fat. Stir in tomatoes with juice, oregano, salt, cumin and pepper. Spoon into 11×7-inch casserole. Sprinkle cheese over casserole; arrange tortilla chips over cheese. Bake 10 to 15 minutes or until cheese melts.

3. Combine sour cream and chilies; mix until well blended. Drop by tablespoonfuls onto baked casserole. Sprinkle with cilantro. *Makes 6 servings*

Mexi-Tortilla Casserole

Saucy Tropical Turkey

3 to 4 turkey thighs, skin removed (about 2½ pounds)
2 tablespoons vegetable oil
1 small onion, halved and sliced
1 can (20 ounces) pineapple chunks, drained
1 red bell pepper, cubed
⅔ cup apricot preserves
3 tablespoons soy sauce
1 teaspoon grated lemon peel
1 teaspoon ground ginger
¼ cup cold water
2 tablespoons cornstarch
Hot cooked rice

Slow Cooker Directions

1. Rinse turkey and pat dry. Heat oil in large skillet over medium-high heat; brown turkey on all sides. Place onion in slow cooker. Transfer turkey to slow cooker; top with pineapple and bell pepper.

2. Combine preserves, soy sauce, lemon peel and ginger in small bowl; mix well. Spoon over turkey. Cover; cook on LOW 6 to 7 hours.

3. Remove turkey from slow cooker; keep warm. Blend water and cornstarch until smooth; stir into slow cooker. Cook, uncovered, on HIGH 15 minutes or until sauce is slightly thickened. Adjust seasonings. Return turkey to slow cooker; cook until hot. Serve with rice. *Makes 6 servings*

Prep Time: 15 minutes
Cook Time: 6½ to 7½ hours

Saucy Tropical Turkey

Tuna Tomato Casserole

2 cans (6 ounces each) tuna, drained
1 cup reduced-fat mayonnaise
1 small onion, finely chopped
¼ teaspoon salt
¼ teaspoon black pepper
1 package (12 ounces) uncooked wide egg noodles
8 to 10 plum tomatoes, sliced ¼ inch thick
1 cup (4 ounces) shredded Cheddar or mozzarella cheese

1. Preheat oven to 375°F.

2. Combine tuna, mayonnaise, onion, salt and pepper in medium bowl. Mix well and set aside.

3. Prepare noodles according to package directions, cooking just until tender. Drain noodles and return to pan.

4. Add tuna mixture to noodles; stir until well blended.

5. Layer half of noodle mixture, half of tomatoes and half of cheese in 13×9-inch baking dish. Press down slightly. Repeat layers with remaining ingredients.

6. Bake 20 minutes or until cheese is melted and casserole is heated through.

Makes 6 servings

tip

For those who want a spicier flavor, serve this casserole with red or green hot pepper sauce.

Tuna Tomato Casserole

healthy eating

BLT Cukes

½ **cup finely chopped lettuce**
½ **cup finely chopped baby spinach**
 3 **slices crisp-cooked and crumbled bacon**
¼ **cup diced tomato**
1 ½ **tablespoons reduced-fat or nonfat mayonnaise**
¼ **teaspoon black pepper**
   Pinch salt
 1 **large cucumber**
   Minced parsley or green onion

1. Combine lettuce, spinach, bacon, tomato, mayonnaise, pepper and salt; set aside.

2. Peel cucumber. Trim off ends; cut in half lengthwise.

3. Using spoon, scoop out and discard seeds. Spoon lettuce mixture into cucumber halves. Sprinkle with parsley. Cut into 2-inch pieces.   *Makes 8 to 10 pieces*

Note: Make these snacks when cucumbers are plentiful and large enough to easily hollow out with a spoon. You can make these up to 12 hours ahead of time and chill until ready to serve.

BLT Cukes

Sub on the Run

2 hard rolls (2 ounces each), split into halves
4 tomato slices
14 turkey pepperoni slices
2 ounces fat-free oven-roasted turkey breast
¼ cup (1 ounce) shredded part-skim mozzarella or reduced-fat sharp Cheddar cheese
1 cup packaged coleslaw mix or shredded lettuce
¼ medium green bell pepper, thinly sliced (optional)
2 tablespoons prepared fat-free Italian salad dressing

Top each bottom half of rolls with 2 tomato slices, 7 pepperoni slices, 1 ounce turkey, 2 tablespoons cheese, ½ cup coleslaw mix and half of bell pepper slices, if desired. Drizzle each half with salad dressing. Top with roll tops. To serve, cut into halves, if desired.   *Makes 2 servings*

tip

After these subs are assembled, wrap them tightly in plastic wrap and refrigerate them. Pack them in lunch bags or boxes along with plenty of napkins. If the sandwiches won't be eaten for a few hours, add ice packs or bottles of frozen water. By the time lunch rolls around, the water bottles will be thawed.

Sub on the Run

Turkey Meat Loaf

1 tablespoon vegetable oil
¾ cup chopped onion
½ cup chopped celery
1 clove garlic, minced
⅔ cup fat-free reduced-sodium chicken broth or water
½ cup uncooked bulgur wheat
1 pound 93% lean ground turkey
½ cup cholesterol-free egg substitute
8 tablespoons chili sauce, divided
1 tablespoon reduced-sodium soy sauce
¼ teaspoon ground cumin
¼ teaspoon paprika
¼ teaspoon black pepper

1. Heat oil in small saucepan over medium heat. Add onion, celery and garlic; cook and stir 3 minutes. Add broth and bulgur. Bring to a boil. Reduce heat to low; cover and simmer 10 to 15 minutes or until bulgur is tender and all liquid is absorbed. Transfer to large bowl; cool to lukewarm.

2. Preheat oven to 375°F. Add turkey, egg substitute, 6 tablespoons chili sauce, soy sauce, cumin, paprika and pepper. Mix until well blended.

3. Pat turkey mixture into greased 8½×4½-inch loaf pan. Top with remaining 2 tablespoons chili sauce.

4. Bake meat loaf about 45 minutes or until until internal temperature reaches 165°F. Let stand 10 minutes; drain excess liquid. Remove from pan; cut into 10 slices.

Makes 5 servings

Variation: If you don't have a loaf pan of the proper size, the turkey mixture may be shaped into an 8½×4½-inch loaf in a 13×9-inch baking pan.

Turkey Meat Loaf

Silly Spaghetti Casserole

Nonstick cooking spray
8 ounces uncooked spaghetti, broken in half
¼ cup finely grated Parmesan cheese
¼ cup cholesterol-free egg substitute
¾ pound lean ground turkey or 90% lean ground beef
⅓ cup chopped onion
2 cups pasta sauce
½ (10-ounce) package frozen cut spinach, thawed and squeezed dry
¾ cup (3 ounces) shredded part-skim mozzarella cheese
1 green or yellow bell pepper, cored and seeded

1. Preheat oven to 350°F. Spray 8-inch square baking dish with nonstick cooking spray.

2. Cook spaghetti according to package directions, omitting salt and oil; drain. Return spaghetti to saucepan; cool slightly Add Parmesan cheese and egg substitute; toss. Place in prepared baking dish.

3. Spray large nonstick skillet with cooking spray. Brown turkey and onion in skillet over medium-high heat, stirring to break up meat. Drain fat. Stir in pasta sauce and spinach. Spoon on top of spaghetti mixture.

4. Sprinkle with mozzarella cheese. Use small cookie cutter to cut decorative shapes from bell pepper. Arrange on top of cheese. Cover with foil. Bake 40 to 45 minutes or until bubbling. Let stand 10 minutes. Cut into squares. *Makes 6 servings*

Silly Spaghetti Casserole

Tuna Schooners

2 cans (3 ounces each) light tuna packed in water, drained
½ cup finely chopped apple
⅓ cup reduced-fat ranch salad dressing
¼ cup shredded carrot
2 English muffins, split and lightly toasted
8 triangular-shaped baked whole wheat crackers or
   triangular-shaped tortilla chips

1. Combine tuna, apple, dressing and carrot in medium bowl; stir until blended.

2. Spread ¼ of tuna mixture onto each muffin half. Stand 2 crackers and press firmly into tuna mixture on each muffin half to form 'sails.'   *Makes 4 servings*

SPAM™ Skillet Casserole

2 baking potatoes, cut into ⅛-inch slices
1 (12-ounce) can SPAM® Lite, cubed
1 cup *each* thinly sliced carrots and onion
½ cup thinly sliced celery
2 cloves garlic, minced
2 tablespoons all-purpose flour
1 teaspoon coarsely ground black pepper
¾ teaspoon dried thyme leaves
1 (16-ounce) can no-salt-added green beans, drained
1 (16-ounce) can no-salt-added whole tomatoes, drained and
   chopped
1 (5½-ounce) can no-salt-added vegetable juice cocktail
   Butter-flavored nonstick cooking spray

Cook potatoes in boiling water 3 minutes or until crisp-tender. Drain. In large skillet, cook SPAM® until browned; remove from skillet. Add carrots to skillet; sauté 4 to 5 minutes. Add onion, celery and garlic; sauté until tender. Combine flour, pepper and thyme. Stir flour mixture into vegetable mixture; cook 1 minute, stirring constantly. Add SPAM®, green beans, tomatoes and vegetable juice cocktail. Bring to a boil. Reduce heat; simmer 5 minutes, stirring occasionally. Remove skillet from heat; arrange potato slices on top. Spray potato slices with cooking spray. Broil 6 inches from heat source 10 minutes or until golden.   *Makes 6 servings*

Tuna Schooners

Ground Beef, Spinach and Barley Soup

¾ pound 95% lean ground beef
4 cups water
1 can (14½ ounces) no-salt-added stewed tomatoes, undrained
1½ cups thinly sliced carrots
1 cup chopped onion
½ cup quick-cooking barley
1½ teaspoons beef bouillon granules
1½ teaspoons dried thyme
1 teaspoon dried oregano
½ teaspoon garlic powder
¼ teaspoon black pepper
⅛ teaspoon salt
3 cups torn stemmed and washed spinach leaves

1. Brown beef in large saucepan over medium heat, stirring to break up meat. Rinse beef under warm water; drain. Return beef to saucepan; add water, tomatoes with juice, carrots, onion, barley, bouillon granules, thyme, oregano, garlic powder, pepper and salt.

2. Bring to a boil over high heat. Reduce heat to medium-low. Cover and simmer 12 to 15 minutes or until barley and vegetables are tender, stirring occasionally. Stir in spinach; cook until spinach starts to wilt. *Makes 4 servings*

Ground Beef, Spinach and Barley Soup

Chicken & Vegetable Tortilla Roll-Ups

1 pound boneless skinless chicken breasts, cooked
1 cup chopped broccoli
1 cup diced carrots
1 can (10¾ ounces) 98% fat-free condensed cream of celery soup,
    undiluted
⅓ cup reduced-fat (2%) milk
½ cup grated Parmesan cheese
6 (10-inch) fat-free flour tortillas

1. Preheat oven to 350°F. Spray 13×9-inch baking dish with nonstick cooking spray; set aside. Cut chicken into 1-inch pieces; set aside.

2. Combine broccoli and carrots in 1-quart microwavable dish. Cover and microwave on HIGH 2 to 3 minutes or until vegetables are crisp-tender; set aside.

3. Combine soup and milk in small saucepan over medium heat; cook and stir 5 minutes. Stir in Parmesan cheese, chicken, broccoli and carrots. Cook 2 minutes or until cheese is melted. Remove from heat.

4. Spoon ¼ cup chicken mixture onto each tortilla. Roll up and place, seam side down, in prepared baking dish. Bake, covered, 20 minutes or until heated through.

Makes 6 servings

Chicken & Vegetable Tortilla Roll-Ups

Rigatoni Salad

12 ounces rigatoni pasta, cooked
1 to 2 cups chopped greens, such as spinach, frisée or any crisp lettuce
1 bag (10 ounces) frozen snowpeas or sugar snap peas, thawed
8 ounces cherry tomatoes, cut into halves
1 medium red or yellow bell pepper, cut into thin strips
½ red onion, cut into thin strips
⅓ cup sliced black olives
⅓ to ½ cup Italian salad dressing
Grated Parmesan cheese (optional)

Combine all ingredients except cheese in large salad bowl. Toss gently to mix and coat all ingredients. Sprinkle with cheese, if desired.   *Makes about 8 servings*

tip

Vary the amounts of each ingredient according to your taste. Substitute steamed green beans (whole or cut) for the peas or add steamed, sliced carrots, zucchini or yellow squash.

Rigatoni Salad

Hash Brown Breakfast Casserole

3 cups frozen shredded hash brown potatoes
1½ cups (6 ounces) finely chopped extra-lean ham
¾ cup (3 ounces) shredded reduced-fat Cheddar cheese
¼ cup sliced green onions
1 can (12 ounces) evaporated fat-free milk
1 tablespoon all-purpose flour
1 cup cholesterol-free egg substitute
½ teaspoon black pepper

1. Lightly coat 8-inch square baking dish with nonstick cooking spray.

2. Layer potatoes, ham, cheese and onions in dish. Gradually whisk milk into flour in small bowl. Stir in egg substitute and pepper. Pour over potato mixture. Cover and refrigerate 4 to 24 hours.

3. Preheat oven to 350°F. Bake, uncovered, 55 to 60 minutes or until knife inserted into center comes out clean. Remove from oven; let stand 10 minutes before serving.

Makes 6 servings

Prep Time: 10 minutes
Chill Time: 4 hours
Bake Time: 55 minutes

Hash Brown Breakfast Casserole

Stanley Sandwiches

½ cup shredded carrot
2 tablespoons reduced-fat ranch salad dressing
½ (12-ounce) focaccia
3 lettuce leaves
6 ounces thinly sliced reduced-fat deli-style roast beef, roast chicken or roast turkey

1. Stir together carrot and salad dressing. Cut focaccia into 3 pieces. Split each piece horizontally. Place lettuce leaves on bottom halves. Top with meat. Spoon carrot mixture on top. Top with remaining focaccia halves. Wrap in plastic wrap.

2. For an on-the-go sandwich, pack in insulated bag with ice pack, if desired.

Makes 3 servings

Meatballs in Cranberry-Barbecue Sauce

1 can (16 ounces) jellied cranberry sauce
½ cup barbecue sauce
1 egg white
1 pound 93% lean ground turkey or lean ground beef
1 green onion, sliced
2 teaspoons grated orange peel
1 teaspoon reduced-sodium soy sauce
¼ teaspoon black pepper
Nonstick cooking spray

Slow Cooker Directions

1. Combine cranberry sauce and barbecue sauce in slow cooker. Cover; cook on HIGH 20 to 30 minutes or until mixture is hot.

2. Meanwhile, beat egg white in medium bowl. Add turkey, onion, orange peel, soy sauce and pepper; mix until well blended. Shape into 24 balls.

3. Spray large nonstick skillet with nonstick cooking spray. Cook meatballs over medium heat 8 to 10 minutes or until brown and no longer pink in center, turning occasionally. Add to slow cooker; stir gently to coat. Cover; cook on HIGH 3 hours.

Makes 12 appetizer servings

Stanley Sandwich

Surfin' Salmon

⅓ **cup cornflake crumbs**
⅓ **cup cholesterol-free egg substitute**
2 **tablespoons fat-free (skim) milk**
¾ **teaspoon dried dill weed**
⅛ **teaspoon black pepper**
 Dash hot pepper sauce
1 **can (14½ ounces) salmon, drained and skin and bones removed**
 Nonstick cooking spray
1 **teaspoon olive oil**
6 **tablespoons tartar sauce**
5 **small pimiento pieces**

1. Combine cornflake crumbs, egg substitute, milk, dill weed, black pepper and hot pepper sauce in large mixing bowl. Add salmon; mix well.

2. Shape salmon mixture into 5 large egg-shaped balls. Flatten each into ¾-inch-thick oval. Pinch one end of each oval to make tail shape for each fish.

3. Spray large nonstick skillet with cooking spray. Add fish to skillet; cook 2 to 3 minutes over medium-high heat or until lightly browned. Turn fish over. Add oil to skillet. Continue cooking 2 to 3 minutes or until firm and lightly browned.

4. Place small drop tartar sauce and pimiento on each fish to make "eye." Serve with remaining tartar sauce, if desired. *Makes 5 servings*

Tip: For a tasty side dish of seaplants, serve fish on a bed of shredded Romaine lettuce and matchstick-size cucumber slices.

Surfin' Salmon

Shotgun Billy's Turkey Chili with Black Beans

1 can (28 ounces) tomatoes, undrained, coarsely chopped
1 cup coarsely chopped onion
1 red bell pepper, chopped
2 cloves garlic, minced
2 fresh jalapeño peppers,* seeded, minced
1 tablespoon chili powder
1½ teaspoons ground cumin
1½ teaspoons ground coriander
½ teaspoon dried oregano leaves
½ teaspoon dried marjoram leaves
¼ teaspoon crushed red pepper flakes
¼ teaspoon ground cinnamon
2 cups cooked turkey, cut into ½-inch cubes
1 can (16 ounces) black beans, drained, rinsed
½ cup coarsely chopped fresh cilantro
4 tablespoons shredded reduced-fat Cheddar cheese

*Jalapeño peppers can sting and irritate the skin; wear rubber or plastic gloves when handling peppers and do not touch eyes. Wash hands after handling.

1. Combine tomatoes with juice, onion, bell pepper, garlic and jalapeño peppers in 3-quart microwave-safe dish. Stir in chili powder, cumin, coriander, oregano, marjoram, pepper flakes and cinnamon; cover.

2. Microwave at HIGH (100% power) 10 minutes, stirring once after 5 minutes. Stir in turkey and beans; cover. Microwave at HIGH 4 minutes more or until heated through; stir in cilantro. To serve, ladle into bowls; sprinkle each serving with 1 tablespoon cheese.
Makes 4 servings

Favorite recipe from **National Turkey Federation**

Shotgun Billy's Turkey Chili with Black Beans

Chicken Roll-Ups

2½ cups marinara sauce*
4 (4 ounces each) boneless skinless chicken breasts
2 cups baby spinach leaves
4 slices (1 ounce each) low-moisture, part-skim mozzarella cheese
4 tablespoons grated Parmesan cheese

*You may use frozen sauce or jarred sauce.

1. Preheat oven to 400°F. Spray baking dish with nonstick cooking spray. Coat bottom of baking dish with 1 cup marinara sauce.

2. Place one chicken breast between 2 sheets of plastic wrap on cutting board. Pound with rolling pin or meat mallet until chicken is about ¼ inch thick. Repeat with remaining chicken breasts.

3. Press ½ cup spinach leaves on each chicken breast. Place 1 slice mozzarella cheese on each and roll up tightly, pressing firmly. Place rolls, seam sides down, in prepared baking dish. Cover with remaining marinara sauce.

4. Cover with foil; bake 35 minutes. Uncover and bake 10 minutes more or until chicken is no longer pink inside. Garnish each serving with 1 tablespoon grated Parmesan cheese. *Makes 4 servings*

Chicken Roll-Up

Tuna Melt

**1 can (12 ounces) chunk albacore tuna packed in water, drained
and flaked**
1½ cups coleslaw mix
3 tablespoons sliced green onions
3 tablespoons reduced-fat mayonnaise
1 tablespoon Dijon mustard
1 teaspoon dried dill weed
4 English muffins, split and lightly toasted
⅓ cup shredded reduced-fat Cheddar cheese

1. Preheat broiler. Combine tuna, coleslaw mix and green onions in medium bowl. Combine mayonnaise, mustard and dill weed in small bowl. Stir mayonnaise mixture into tuna mixture. Spread tuna mixture onto muffin halves. Place on broiler pan.

2. Broil 4 inches from heat 3 to 4 minutes or until heated through. Sprinkle with cheese. Broil 1 to 2 minutes more or until cheese melts. *Makes 4 servings*

tip

Canned albacore or white tuna is available in three grades: solid or fancy, chunk, and grated or flaked. The solid grade indicates that the tuna is in large pieces, chunk in smaller pieces and grated in bits and pieces. For a low-fat option, choose tuna packed in water.

Tuna Melts

Tortellini Teasers

Zesty Tomato Sauce (recipe follows)
½ (9-ounce) package refrigerated cheese tortellini
1 large red or green bell pepper, cut into 1-inch pieces
2 medium carrots, peeled and sliced ½ inch thick
1 medium zucchini, sliced ½ inch thick
12 medium fresh mushrooms
12 cherry tomatoes

1. Prepare Zesty Tomato Sauce; keep warm.

2. Cook tortellini according to package directions; drain.

3. Alternate tortellini and vegetable pieces on wooden skewers. Serve as dippers with tomato sauce.   *Makes 6 servings*

Zesty Tomato Sauce

1 can (15 ounces) tomato purée
2 tablespoons finely chopped onion
2 tablespoons chopped fresh parsley
1 teaspoon dried oregano
¼ teaspoon dried thyme
¼ teaspoon salt
⅛ teaspoon black pepper
Carrot curl (optional)

Combine tomato purée, onion, parsley, oregano and thyme in small saucepan. Heat thoroughly, stirring occasionally. Stir in salt and pepper. Garnish with carrot curl, if desired.

Tortellini Teasers

Mandarin Orange Chicken

4 boneless skinless chicken breasts (1 pound)
⅛ teaspoon salt
⅛ teaspoon black pepper
  Nonstick cooking spray
½ cup finely chopped onion (about 1 small)
½ cup orange juice
2 teaspoons minced fresh ginger
1 teaspoon sugar
2 teaspoons cornstarch
¼ cup cold water
1 can (11 ounces) mandarin orange segments, drained
2 to 3 tablespoons finely chopped fresh cilantro
2 cups hot cooked rice
  Additional fresh cilantro (optional)

1. Pound chicken slightly between 2 pieces of plastic wrap to ¼-inch thickness using flat side of meat mallet or rolling pin. Broil chicken, 6 inches from heat source, 7 to 8 minutes on each side until chicken is no longer pink in center. Or, grill chicken, on covered grill over medium-hot coals, 10 minutes on each side or until chicken is no longer pink in center. Sprinkle with salt and pepper.

2. Spray medium nonstick saucepan with cooking spray; heat over medium heat until hot. Add onion; cook and stir about 5 minutes or until tender. Add orange juice, ginger and sugar. Bring to a boil.

3. Combine cornstarch and water in small bowl until smooth; add to onion mixture, stirring until thickened. Boil 1 minute, stirring constantly. Stir in orange segments and cilantro. Serve chicken over rice; top with sauce. Garnish as desired.

Makes 4 servings

Mandarin Orange Chicken

Señor Nacho Dip

½ package (4 ounces) fat-free cream cheese, cubed
½ cup (2 ounces) shredded reduced-fat Cheddar cheese
¼ cup mild or medium chunky salsa
2 teaspoons reduced-fat (2%) milk
Baked tortilla chips and assorted fresh vegetable dippers
Hot peppers and cilantro (optional)

1. Combine cream cheese and Cheddar cheese in small saucepan; cook and stir over low heat until melted. Stir in salsa and milk; heat thoroughly, stirring occasionally.

2. Transfer dip to small serving bowl. Serve with tortilla chips and vegetables. Garnish with hot peppers and cilantro, if desired.

Makes 4 snack or 3 lunch servings

Olé Dip: Substitute reduced-fat Monterey Jack cheese or reduced-fat taco cheese for Cheddar cheese.

Spicy Mustard Dip: Omit tortilla chips. Substitute 2 teaspoons spicy brown mustard or honey mustard for salsa. Serve with fresh vegetable dippers or pretzels.

tip

Reduced-fat cream cheese may be substituted for the fat-free variety called for in this recipe.

Señor Nacho Dip

Broccoli, Chicken and Rice Casserole

1 box UNCLE BEN'S CHEF'S RECIPE® Broccoli Rice Au Gratin Supreme
2 cups boiling water
4 boneless, skinless chicken breasts (about 1 pound)
¼ teaspoon garlic powder
2 cups frozen broccoli
1 cup (4 ounces) reduced-fat shredded Cheddar cheese

1. Heat oven to 425°F. In 13×9-inch baking pan, combine rice and contents of seasoning packet. Add boiling water; mix well. Add chicken; sprinkle with garlic powder. Cover and bake 30 minutes.

2. Add broccoli and cheese; continue to bake, covered, 8 to 10 minutes or until chicken is no longer pink in center. *Makes 4 servings*

Mexican Turkey Chili Mac

1 pound ground turkey
1 package (1¼ ounces) reduced-sodium taco seasoning mix
1 can (14½ ounces) reduced-sodium stewed tomatoes
1 can (11 ounces) corn with red and green peppers, undrained
1½ cups cooked elbow macaroni, without salt, drained
1 ounce low-salt corn chips, crushed
½ cup shredded reduced-fat Cheddar cheese

1. In large nonstick skillet, over medium-high heat, sauté turkey 5 to 6 minutes or until no longer pink; drain. Stir in taco seasoning, tomatoes, corn and macaroni. Reduce heat to medium and cook 4 to 5 minutes until heated throughout.

2. Sprinkle corn chips over meat mixture and top with cheese. Cover and heat 1 to 2 minutes or until cheese is melted. *Makes 6 servings*

*Favorite recipe from **National Turkey Federation***

Broccoli, Chicken and Rice Casserole

Kids' Wraps

4 teaspoons Dijon honey mustard
2 (8-inch) fat-free flour tortillas
2 slices reduced-fat American cheese, cut in half
4 ounces thinly sliced fat-free oven-roasted turkey breast
½ cup shredded carrot (about 1 medium)
3 romaine lettuce leaves, washed and torn into bite-size pieces

1. Spread 2 teaspoons mustard evenly over 1 tortilla.

2. Top with half of cheese, turkey, carrot and lettuce.

3. Roll up tortilla; cut in half. Repeat with remaining ingredients.   *Makes 2 servings*

Mexican Rice and Turkey Bake

1 bag SUCCESS® Rice
   Vegetable cooking spray
3 cups chopped cooked turkey
1 can (10 ounces) tomatoes with chilies, undrained*
1 can (12 ounces) Mexican-style corn with sweet peppers, drained
1 cup fat-free sour cream
½ cup (2 ounces) shredded low-fat Cheddar cheese

*Or, use 1 can (14½ ounces) stewed tomatoes. Add 1 can (4 ounces) drained chopped mild green chilies.

Microwave Directions

Prepare rice according to package directions.

Spray 1½-quart microwave-safe casserole with cooking spray; set aside. Combine rice, turkey, tomatoes and corn in large bowl; mix well. Spoon into prepared casserole. Microwave on HIGH until hot and bubbly, 8 to 10 minutes, stirring after 5 minutes. Top with sour cream and cheese.   *Makes 6 servings*

Conventional Oven: Assemble casserole as directed. Spoon into ovenproof 1½-quart casserole sprayed with vegetable cooking spray. Bake at 350°F until thoroughly heated, 15 to 20 minutes.

Kids' Wrap

Sausage Vegetable Rotini Soup

Nonstick cooking spray
6 ounces bulk pork sausage
1 cup chopped onion
1 cup chopped green bell pepper
3 cups water
1 can (14½ ounces) diced tomatoes, undrained
¼ cup ketchup
2 teaspoons reduced-sodium beef granules
2 teaspoons chili powder
4 ounces uncooked tri-colored rotini
1 cup frozen corn, thawed

1. Heat Dutch oven over medium-high heat until hot. Spray with nonstick cooking spray. Brown sausage about 3 minutes, stirring to break up meat. Drain fat. Add onion and bell pepper; cook and stir 3 to 4 minutes or until onion is translucent.

2. Add water, tomatoes with juice, ketchup, beef granules and chili powder; bring to a boil over high heat. Stir in pasta; return to a boil. Reduce heat; simmer, uncovered, 12 minutes. Stir in corn; cook 2 minutes. *Makes 4 servings*

Wacky Tomato Macky

1 box (7 ounces) elbow macaroni
**2 cans (14½ ounces each) diced tomatoes seasoned with basil,
    garlic and oregano, undrained**
⅛ teaspoon black pepper
1 teaspoon corn oil
1 tablespoon grated Parmesan cheese

1. Cook macaroni according to package directions, omitting any salt or oil. Drain and return to saucepan.

2. Add tomatoes, pepper and oil. Cook, uncovered, over medium-low heat 15 minutes or until tomatoes are hot and some of the liquid has evaporated.

3. Serve with Parmesan cheese. *Makes 12 side-dish servings*

Sausage Vegetable Rotini Soup

Tropical Chicken Salad Pockets

3 cups diced cooked chicken*
1 can (20 ounces) pineapple chunks in juice, drained, juice reserved
3 green onions, thinly sliced
2 tablespoons chopped fresh cilantro
   Tropical Dressing (recipe follows)
4 pocket breads, cut in half
   Lettuce leaves

*Use home-roasted chicken or ready-to-eat roasted chicken from the supermarket or deli.

In bowl, place chicken, pineapple, green onions and cilantro. Pour dressing over chicken mixture and toss to mix. Line each pocket bread with lettuce leaf; fill with chicken salad.   *Makes 4 servings*

Tropical Dressing: In small bowl, mix together ½ cup reduced-fat mayonnaise, 1 tablespoon lime juice, 1 tablespoon reserved pineapple juice, 1 teaspoon sugar, 1 teaspoon curry powder, ½ teaspoon salt and ¼ teaspoon grated lime peel. Makes about ⅔ cup dressing.

*Favorite recipe from **Delmarva Poultry Industry, Inc.***

tip

For added fiber and nutrients, you may substitute whole wheat pocket breads in this recipe.

Tropical Chicken Salad Pockets

Cincinnati 5-Way Chili

¾ **pound ground turkey**
1 **cup chopped onion, divided**
3 **cloves garlic, minced**
1 **can (8 ounces) reduced-sodium tomato sauce**
¾ **cup water**
1 **to 2 tablespoons chili powder**
1 **tablespoon unsweetened cocoa powder**
1 **to 2 teaspoons cider vinegar**
1 **teaspoon ground cinnamon**
½ **teaspoon ground allspice**
½ **teaspoon paprika**
1 **bay leaf**
⅛ **teaspoon ground cloves (optional)**
   Salt and black pepper
8 **ounces hot cooked spaghetti**
½ **cup (2 ounces) shredded fat-free Cheddar cheese**
½ **cup red kidney beans, rinsed and drained**

1. Brown turkey in medium saucepan over medium heat about 5 minutes, stirring to break up meat. Drain fat. Add ½ cup onion and garlic; cook and stir about 5 minutes or until onion is tender.

2. Add tomato sauce, water, chili powder, cocoa, vinegar, cinnamon, allspice, paprika, bay leaf and cloves, if desired. Bring to a boil. Reduce heat and simmer, covered, 15 minutes, stirring occasionally. If thicker consistency is desired, simmer, uncovered, about 5 minutes more. Discard bay leaf; season to taste with salt and pepper.

3. Spoon spaghetti into bowls; spoon sauce over top and sprinkle with remaining ½ cup onion, cheese and beans. *Makes 4 main-dish servings*

Chicken & Dumplings Casserole

¾ pound chicken tenders, cut into bite-size pieces
6 new red or Yukon gold potatoes, quartered (about ½ pound)
1 cup baby carrots
1 cup frozen green peas, thawed
2 tablespoons all-purpose flour
¼ teaspoon salt
¼ teaspoon black pepper
1 can (about 14 ounces) fat-free, reduced-sodium chicken broth
½ cup reduced-fat biscuit baking mix
¼ cup water

1. Lightly spray 9½-inch glass microwavable pie plate with nonstick cooking spray.

2. Place chicken, potatoes, carrots, peas, flour, salt and pepper in large resealable bag; seal bag. Shake to coat ingredients with flour and seasonings. Place chicken and vegetables into prepared pie plate, distributing evenly. Add chicken broth. Cover with 10-inch round of waxed paper. Microwave on HIGH 20 minutes.

3. Meanwhile, combine biscuit mix and water in bowl; mix lightly with fork. Set aside.

4. Preheat oven to 400°F.

5. Remove pie plate from microwave. Discard waxed paper. Drop teaspoons of biscuit dough over chicken mixture.

6. Bake 10 minutes or until dumplings are puffed and cooked through. Let cool 5 minutes before serving. *Makes 6 servings*

super snacks

Finger-Lickin' Chicken Salad

½ cup diced roasted skinless chicken breast
½ stalk celery, cut into 1-inch pieces
¼ cup drained mandarin orange segments
¼ cup red seedless grapes
2 tablespoons fat-free, sugar-free lemon yogurt
1 tablespoon reduced-fat mayonnaise
¼ teaspoon reduced-sodium soy sauce
⅛ teaspoon pumpkin pie spice or cinnamon

1. Toss together chicken, celery, oranges and grapes in plastic container; cover.

2. For dipping sauce, combine yogurt, mayonnaise, soy sauce and pumpkin pie spice in small bowl. Place in small plastic container; cover.

3. Pack chicken mixture and dipping sauce in insulated bag with ice pack. To serve, dip chicken mixture into dipping sauce.   *Makes 1 serving*

Serving Suggestion: Thread the chicken on wooden skewers alternately with celery, oranges and grapes. The salad and the skewers are ideal for a school lunch.

Finger-Lickin' Chicken Salad

Jiggly Banana Split

1 banana
3 gelatin snack cups, any flavors (3 ounces each)
2 tablespoons whipped topping
  Colored sprinkles
1 maraschino cherry

1. Peel banana and cut in half lengthwise. Place banana in serving dish, separating halves. Unmold gelatin snack cups by dipping partially in warm water for a few seconds. Slide gelatin from cups; place between banana halves.

2. Top with dollops of whipped topping, sprinkles and cherry.   *Makes 1 serving*

Prep Time: 5 minutes

Peanut Butter-Pineapple Celery Sticks

½ cup low-fat (1%) cottage cheese
½ cup reduced-fat peanut butter
½ cup crushed pineapple in juice, drained
12 (3-inch-long) celery sticks

Combine cottage cheese and peanut butter in food processor. Blend until smooth. Stir in pineapple. Stuff celery sticks with mixture.   *Makes 6 servings*

Serving Suggestion: You can substitute two medium apples, cored and sliced, for the celery.

Jiggly Banana Split

Original Ranch® & Cheddar Bread

1 cup HIDDEN VALLEY® The Original Ranch® Dressing
2 cups (8 ounces) shredded sharp Cheddar cheese
1 whole loaf (1 pound) French bread (not sour dough)

Stir together dressing and cheese. Cut bread in half lengthwise. Place on a broiler pan and spread dressing mixture evenly over cut side of each half. Broil until lightly brown. Cut each half into 8 pieces. *Makes 16 pieces*

Peanut Butter Crispy Treats

4 cups toasted rice cereal
1¾ cups "M&M's"® Milk Chocolate Mini Baking Bits
4 cups mini marshmallows
½ cup creamy peanut butter
¼ cup butter or margarine
⅛ teaspoon salt

Combine cereal and "M&M's"® Milk Chocolate Mini Baking Bits in lightly greased baking pan; set aside. Melt marshmallows, peanut butter, butter and salt in heavy saucepan over low heat, stirring occasionally until mixture is smooth. Pour melted mixture over cereal mixture, tossing lightly until thoroughly coated. Gently shape into 1½-inch balls with buttered fingers. Place on waxed paper; cool at room temperature until set. Store in tightly covered container. *Makes about 3 dozen*

Variation: After cereal mixture is thoroughly coated, press lightly into greased 13×9×2-inch pan. Cool completely; cut into bars. Makes 24 bars.

Original Ranch® & Cheddar Bread

Warm Peanut-Caramel Dip

¼ cup reduced-fat peanut butter
2 tablespoons fat-free caramel ice cream topping
2 tablespoons fat-free (skim) milk
1 large apple, thinly sliced
4 large pretzel rods, broken in half

1. Combine peanut butter, caramel topping and milk in small saucepan. Heat over low heat, stirring constantly, until mixture is melted and warm.

2. Serve dip with apple slices and pretzel rods.   *Makes 4 servings*

Microwave Directions: Combine all ingredients except apple slices and pretzel rods in small microwavable dish. Microwave on MEDIUM (50%) 1 minute; stir well. Microwave an additional minute or until mixture is melted and warm. Serve dip with apple slices and pretzel rods.

tip

This dip is also great served with banana slices, pear slices, baked reduced-fat crackers and graham crackers.

Warm Peanut-Caramel Dip

Maraschino-Lemonade Pops

1 (10-ounce) jar maraschino cherries
8 (3-ounce) paper cups
1 (12-ounce) can frozen pink lemonade concentrate, partly thawed
¼ cup water
8 popsicle sticks

Drain cherries, reserving juice. Place one whole cherry in each paper cup. Coarsely chop remaining cherries. Add chopped cherries, lemonade concentrate, water and reserved juice to container of blender or food processor; blend until smooth. Fill paper cups with equal amounts of cherry mixture. Freeze several hours or until very slushy. Place popsicle sticks in the center of each cup. Freeze 1 hour longer or until firm. To serve, peel off paper cups.   *Makes 8 servings*

Note: Serve immediately after peeling off paper cups—these pops melt very quickly.

Favorite recipe from **Cherry Marketing Institute**

Chocolate, Peanut Butter & Apple Treats

½ package (8 ounces) reduced-fat or fat-free cream cheese, softened
¼ cup reduced-fat chunky peanut butter
2 tablespoons mini chocolate chips
2 large apples

1. Combine cream cheese, peanut butter and chocolate chips in small bowl; mix well.

2. Cut each apple into quarters; core. Cut each quarter into 3 slices. Spread about 1½ teaspoons of cream cheese mixture over each apple slice.   *Makes 8 servings*

Maraschino-Lemonade Pops

Take-Along Snack Mix

1 tablespoon butter or margarine
2 tablespoons honey
1 cup toasted oat cereal, any flavor
½ cup coarsely broken pecans
½ cup thin pretzel sticks, broken in half
½ cup raisins
1 cup "M&M's"® Chocolate Mini Baking Bits

In large heavy skillet over low heat, melt butter. Add honey; stir until blended. Add cereal, nuts, pretzels and raisins; stir until all pieces are evenly coated. Continue cooking over low heat 10 minutes, stirring frequently. Remove from heat; immediately spread on waxed paper until cool. Add "M&M's"® Chocolate Mini Baking Bits. Store in tightly covered container. *Makes about 3½ cups*

tip

Pack snack mixes in small plastic containers or resealable bags for on-the-go-snacking or school-lunch desserts.

Take-Along Snack Mix

Banana Roll-Ups

¼ cup smooth or crunchy almond butter
2 tablespoons mini chocolate chips
1 to 2 tablespoons milk
1 whole wheat flour tortilla (8 inches)
1 large banana, peeled

1. Combine almond butter, chocolate chips and 1 tablespoon milk in medium microwavable bowl. Microwave on MEDIUM (50% power) 40 seconds. Stir well and repeat if necessary to melt chocolate. Add more milk if necessary for desired consistency.

2. Spread almond butter mixture on tortilla. Place banana on one side of tortilla and roll up tightly. Cut into 8 (1-inch) slices. *Makes 4 servings*

Picnic Pizza Muffins

1 can (12 ounces) refrigerated flaky buttermilk biscuits
¾ pound sweet Italian sausage, removed from casings
½ cup chopped green bell pepper
½ cup canned sliced mushrooms
½ cup pizza sauce
½ cup shredded mozzarella cheese
1 tablespoon *Frank's*® *RedHot*® Original Cayenne Pepper Sauce

1. Preheat oven to 375°F. Separate biscuits; pat into 3-inch circles. Press circles into muffin cups. Fill empty muffin cups halfway with water; set aside.

2. Cook sausage and vegetables in large nonstick skillet over high heat 5 to 8 minutes or until meat is browned, stirring to separate meat. Drain fat. Stir in pizza sauce, cheese and ***Frank's RedHot*** Sauce; mix well.

3. Mound filling into muffin cups, dividing evenly. Bake 20 minutes or until muffins are browned. Serve warm or at room temperature. *Makes 10 servings*

Prep Time: 15 minutes
Cook Time: 25 minutes

Banana Roll-Ups

Peanut Butter-Apple Wraps

¾ cup creamy peanut butter
4 (7-inch) whole wheat flour or spinach tortillas or 8-grain lavash
1 large apple, finely chopped
⅓ cup shredded carrot
⅓ cup low-fat granola without raisins
1 tablespoon toasted wheat germ

Spread peanut butter on one side of each tortilla. Sprinkle each tortilla with ¼ apple, carrot, granola and wheat germ. Roll up tightly; cut each wrap in half. Serve immediately or refrigerate until ready to serve. *Makes 4 servings*

Prep Time: 5 minutes
Chill Time: 2 hours

tip

Peanut Butter-Apple Wraps make a good lunch-box addition. Simply cut each wrap in half, then tightly wrap the halves in plastic wrap.

Peanut Butter-Apple Wraps

Bagelroonies

6 onion bagels
6 tablespoons soft-spread margarine
1 (14-ounce) jar NEWMAN'S OWN® Sockarooni™ Sauce
1 (8-ounce) package Canadian bacon slices
1 (16-ounce) package mozzarella cheese, shredded (2 cups)
Freshly grated Parmesan cheese

Cut bagels in half; spread with margarine. Spoon Newman's Own® Sockarooni sauce onto bagel halves, approximately 3 tablespoons per bagel half. Chop Canadian bacon slices and place over sauce. Sprinkle liberally with shredded mozzarella cheese. If desired, shake grated Parmesan cheese over bagels. Broil until cheese melts and bubbles.   *Makes 6 servings*

Note: If desired, sprinkle with mushrooms, olives or jalapeño peppers.

"Moo-vin" Strawberry Milk Shake

1 pint low-fat, sugar-free vanilla ice cream
1 cup thawed frozen unsweetened strawberries
¼ cup fat-free (skim) milk
¼ teaspoon vanilla

Combine all ingredients in blender container. Cover and blend until smooth. Pour into 2 small glasses. Serve immediately.   *Makes 2 servings*

Quick Pimiento Cheese Snacks

2 ounces reduced-fat cream cheese, softened
½ cup (2 ounces) shredded reduced-fat Cheddar cheese
1 jar (2 ounces) diced pimientos, drained
2 tablespoons finely chopped pecans
½ teaspoon hot pepper sauce
24 (¼-inch-thick) French bread slices or party bread slices

1. Preheat broiler.

2. Combine cream cheese and Cheddar cheese in small bowl; mix well. Stir in pimientos, pecans and pepper sauce.

3. Place bread slices on broiler pan or nonstick baking sheet. Broil 4 inches from heat 1 to 2 minutes or until lightly toasted on both sides.

4. Spread cheese mixture evenly onto bread slices. Broil 1 to 2 minutes or until cheese mixture is hot and bubbly. Transfer to serving plate; garnish, if desired.

Makes 24 servings

Muffin Pizza Italiano

1 sandwich-size English muffin, split, toasted
2 tablespoons CONTADINA® Pizza Squeeze Pizza Sauce
8 slices pepperoni
¼ cup sliced fresh mushrooms
¼ cup (1 ounce) shredded mozzarella cheese

1. Spread muffin halves with pizza sauce. Top with pepperoni, mushrooms and cheese.

2. Bake in preheated 400°F oven for 8 to 10 minutes or until cheese is melted.

Makes 2 servings

Prep Time: 5 minutes
Cook Time: 10 minutes

classroom treats

Cracker Toffee

72 buttery round crackers
1 cup (2 sticks) unsalted butter
1 cup packed brown sugar
¼ teaspoon salt
2½ cups semisweet chocolate chips
2 cups chopped pecans

1. Preheat oven to 375°F. Line 17×12-inch jelly-roll pan with heavy-duty foil. Spray generously with nonstick cooking spray. Arrange crackers in pan; set aside.

2. Combine butter, brown sugar and salt in heavy medium saucepan. Heat over medium heat until butter melts, stirring frequently. Increase heat to high; boil 3 minutes without stirring. Pour butter mixture evenly onto crackers; spread to cover.

3. Bake 5 minutes. Remove from oven; immediately sprinkle chocolate chips evenly onto crackers. Spread melted chocolate to cover crackers. Sprinkle with pecans, pressing down. Cool to room temperature. Refrigerate 2 hours. Break crackers into chunks to serve. *Makes 24 servings*

Variation: Substitute 1 cup peanut butter chips for 1 cup chocolate chips and 2 cups lightly salted, coarsely chopped peanuts for 2 cups chopped pecans.

Cracker Toffee

Sweet Treat Tortillas

4 (7- to 8-inch) flour tortillas
½ package (4 ounces) Neufchâtel cheese, softened
¼ cup strawberry or other flavor fruit spread or preserves
1 medium banana, peeled and chopped

1. Spread each tortilla with 1 ounce Neufchatel cheese and 1 tablespoon fruit spread; top with ¼ of banana.

2. Roll up tortillas; cut crosswise into thirds.   *Makes 4 servings*

Tip: Substitute your favorite chopped fruit for banana.

Cinnamon-Spice Treats: Omit fruit spread and banana. Mix small amounts of sugar, ground cinnamon and nutmeg to taste into Neufchâtel cheese; spread evenly onto tortillas. Sprinkle lightly with desired amount of chopped pecans or walnuts. Top with chopped fruit, if desired; roll up. Cut crosswise into thirds. Makes 4 servings.

Orange Yogurt Dip for Fresh Fruit

1 carton (8 ounces) low-fat plain yogurt
2 tablespoons honey
   Grated peel of ½ SUNKIST® orange
2 SUNKIST® oranges, peeled and segmented
1 medium unpeeled apple, sliced*
1 medium banana, peeled and cut into chunks*

*Sprinkle cut apple and banana with small amount of orange or lemon juice to prevent fruit from darkening.

In small bowl, combine yogurt, honey and orange peel. Serve as dip with oranges, apple and banana.   *Makes 4 (2-ounce) servings*

Tip: To serve in orange shells, cut oranges in half crosswise. Ream juice from both halves. Scrape shells clean with spoon. Cut small slice off bottom of shells so orange halves are level. Fill as desired. Shells can be made and frozen ahead, to be used at a later date. (Save juice for drinking or use in other recipes.)

Sweet Treat Tortillas

Spicy, Fruity Popcorn Mix

4 cups lightly salted popped popcorn
2 cups corn cereal squares
1 ½ cups dried pineapple wedges
1 package (6 ounces) dried fruit bits
  Butter-flavored nonstick cooking spray
2 tablespoons sugar
1 tablespoon ground cinnamon
1 cup yogurt-covered raisins

1. Preheat oven to 350°F. Combine popcorn, cereal, pineapple and fruit bits in large bowl; mix lightly. Transfer to 15×10-inch jelly-roll pan. Spray mixture generously with cooking spray.

2. Combine sugar and cinnamon in small bowl. Sprinkle ½ of the sugar mixture over popcorn mixture; toss lightly to coat. Spray mixture again with additional cooking spray. Add remaining sugar mixture; mix lightly.

3. Bake 10 minutes, stirring after 5 minutes. Cool completely in pan on wire rack. Add raisins; mix lightly.   *Makes about 8½ cups snack mix*

Cherry Fizz

1 cup cherry juice blend
2 cups frozen unsweetened tart cherries
1 (6-ounce) can frozen pink or regular lemonade concentrate,
  undiluted
6 to 8 ice cubes
1 (12-ounce) can lemon-lime carbonated beverage, chilled
  Orange and lime slices, for garnish

Put cherry juice blend and frozen cherries in a blender container; purée until smooth. Add lemonade concentrate and ice cubes; blend until smooth. Pour mixture into a 2-quart pitcher. Stir in lemon-lime carbonated beverage. Garnish with orange and lime slices. Serve immediately.   *Makes 6 (8-ounce) servings*

Favorite recipe from **Cherry Marketing Institute**

Spicy, Fruity Popcorn Mix

Berry Surprise Cupcakes

1 package DUNCAN HINES® Moist Deluxe® White Cake Mix
1⅓ cups water
3 egg whites
2 tablespoons vegetable oil
3 sheets (½ ounce each) strawberry chewy fruit snacks
1 container DUNCAN HINES® Vanilla Frosting
2 pouches (about 1 ounce each) chewy fruit snack shapes, for garnish (optional)

1. Preheat oven to 350°F. Place paper liners in 24 (2½-inch) muffin cups.

2. Combine cake mix, water, egg whites and oil in large bowl. Beat at low speed with electric mixer until moistened. Beat at medium speed 2 minutes. Fill each liner half full with batter.

3. Cut three fruit snack sheets into 9 equal pieces. (You will have 3 extra squares.) Place each fruit snack piece on top of batter in each cup. Pour remaining batter equally over each. Bake at 350°F for 18 to 23 minutes or until toothpick inserted in centers come out clean. Cool in pans 5 minutes. Remove to cooling racks. Cool completely. Frost cupcakes with Vanilla frosting. Decorate with fruit snack shapes, if desired. *Makes 12 to 16 servings*

Variation: To make a Berry Surprise Cake, prepare cake following package directions. Pour half the batter into prepared 13×9×2-inch pan. Place 4 fruit snack sheets evenly on top. Pour remaining batter over all. Bake and cool as directed on package. Frost and decorate as directed.

Berry Surprise Cupcakes

Dipped, Drizzled & Decorated Pretzels

1 package (12 ounces) chocolate (any flavor) or flavored chips (mint, white chocolate, butterscotch, peanut butter or combination)
24 pretzel rods
Assorted toppings: colored sprinkles, chopped nuts, coconut, toasted coconut, cookie crumbs, colored sugars

Microwave Directions

1. Line baking sheet with waxed paper; place cooling rack on top. Place chips in microwavable bowl. (Be sure bowl and utensils are completely dry.) Microwave on HIGH 1 minute; stir. Microwave at 30-second intervals, stirring after each interval, until chocolate is melted and smooth.

2. Dip one half of each pretzel rod into melted chocolate; sprinkle with or roll in toppings. Drizzle some dipped pretzel rods with contrasting color/flavor of melted chips. (Drizzle melted chocolate from spoon while rotating pretzel, to get even coverage.)

3. Place decorated pretzels on prepared cooling rack; let stand until set. Do not refrigerate.

Makes 2 dozen pretzels

tip

Not only do these decorated pretzels make an ideal classroom treat, but they are a great gift. To arrange a "bouquet" of pretzels, wrap the tops of the pretzels individually in cellophane and place them in a small vase wrapped with a bow. Or, spread a few inches of crinkled paper gift basket filler in the bottom of a smooth-sided 2-quart glass jar. Stand the pretzels, dipped ends up, in the jar and decorate the jar with fabric and ribbon.

Dipped, Drizzled & Decorated Pretzels

Double Chocolate Cranberry Chunkies

1¾ **cups all-purpose flour**
⅓ **cup unsweetened cocoa powder**
½ **teaspoon baking powder**
½ **teaspoon salt**
1 **cup butter, softened**
1 **cup granulated sugar**
½ **cup packed brown sugar**
1 **egg**
1 **teaspoon vanilla**
2 **cups semisweet chocolate chunks or large chocolate chips**
¾ **cup dried cranberries or dried tart cherries**
   Additional granulated sugar

1. Preheat oven to 350°F.

2. Combine flour, cocoa, baking powder and salt in small bowl; set aside. Beat butter, 1 cup granulated sugar and brown sugar in large bowl with electric mixer at medium speed until light and fluffy. Beat in egg and vanilla until well blended. Gradually beat in flour mixture at low speed until blended. Stir in chocolate chunks and cranberries.

3. Drop dough by level ¼ cupfuls onto ungreased cookie sheets, spacing 3 inches apart. Flatten dough until 2 inches in diameter with bottom of glass that has been lightly greased and dipped in additional granulated sugar.

4. Bake 11 to 12 minutes or until cookies are set. Cool cookies 2 minutes on cookie sheets; transfer to wire racks. Cool completely.

Makes about 1 dozen (4-inch) cookies

tip

These giant cookies are great for a special occasion, but for other uses make smaller versions of them. Drop dough by tablespoonfuls as directed in step 3. Flatten dough to 1½ inches. Bake 10 to 11 minutes or until set. Makes about 3 dozen (2½-inch) cookies.

Double Chocolate Cranberry Chunkies

Cinnamon Apple Chips

2 cups unsweetened apple juice
1 cinnamon stick
2 Washington Red Delicious apples

1. In large skillet or saucepan, combine apple juice and cinnamon stick; bring to a low boil while preparing apples.

2. With paring knife, slice off ½ inch from tops and bottoms of apples and discard (or eat). Cut crosswise into ⅛-inch-thick slices, rotating apple as necessary to cut even slices.

3. Drop slices into boiling juice; cook 4 to 5 minutes or until slices appear translucent and lightly golden. Meanwhile, preheat oven to 250°F.

4. With slotted spatula, remove apple slices from juice and pat dry. Arrange slices on wire racks, making sure none overlap. Place racks on middle shelf in oven; bake 30 to 40 minutes until slices are lightly browned and almost dry to touch. Let chips cool on racks completely before storing in airtight container.

Makes about 40 chips

Tip: There is no need to core apples because boiling in juice for several minutes softens core and removes seeds.

Favorite recipe from **Washington Apple Commission**

"Lemon Float" Punch

Juice of 10 to 12 SUNKIST® lemons (2 cups)
¾ cup sugar
4 cups water
1 bottle (2 liters) ginger ale, chilled
1 pint lemon sherbet or frozen vanilla yogurt
Lemon half-cartwheel slices and fresh mint leaves for garnish

Combine lemon juice and sugar; stir to dissolve sugar. Add water; chill. To serve, in large punch bowl, combine lemon mixture and ginger ale. Add small scoops of sherbet, lemon slices and mint. *Makes about 15 cups (thirty 6-ounce servings)*

Cinnamon Apple Chips

Funny-Face Cheese Ball

2 packages (8 ounces each) reduced-fat cream cheese, softened
2 cups (8 ounces) shredded Mexican-blend cheese
1¼ cups shredded carrot, divided
2 tablespoons fat-free (skim) milk
2 teaspoons chili powder
¼ teaspoon ground cumin
¼ teaspoon garlic powder
2 slices pimento-stuffed olives
1 peperoncini pepper
3 slices red or yellow bell pepper
Reduced-fat shredded wheat crackers and celery sticks

1. Beat cream cheese, Mexican-blend cheese, 1 cup shredded carrot, milk, chili powder, cumin and garlic powder in large bowl with electric mixer at medium speed until well blended.

2. Shape mixture into ball. Arrange remaining ¼ cup shredded carrot on top of ball for hair. Use olives for eyes, peperoncini pepper for nose and bell pepper for ears and mouth. Serve immediately or cover and refrigerate until serving time.

3. Serve with crackers and celery sticks.

Makes 24 servings

Prep Time: 15 minutes

Peanut Butter Spread

½ cup part skim ricotta cheese
2 tablespoons peanut butter
1 tablespoon brown sugar
¼ teaspoon cinnamon
4 flour tortillas
1 sliced banana or apple, or jam

Mix ricotta cheese, peanut butter, brown sugar and cinnamon together. Spread equally over tortillas and cover with banana, apple or jam. Roll tortillas. Keep leftover spread refrigerated.

Makes 4 servings

*Favorite recipe from **The Sugar Association, Inc.***

Funny-Face Cheese Ball

Coconutty "M&M's"® Brownies

6 squares (1 ounce each) semi-sweet chocolate
¾ cup granulated sugar
½ cup (1 stick) butter
2 eggs
1 tablespoon vegetable oil
1 teaspoon vanilla extract
1¼ cups all-purpose flour
3 tablespoons unsweetened cocoa powder
1 teaspoon baking powder
½ teaspoon salt
1½ cups "M&M's"® Chocolate Mini Baking Bits, divided
  Coconut Topping (recipe follows)

Preheat oven to 350°F. Lightly grease 8×8×2-inch baking pan; set aside. In small saucepan combine chocolate, sugar and butter over low heat; stir constantly until chocolate is melted. Remove from heat; let cool slightly. In large bowl beat eggs, oil and vanilla; stir in chocolate mixture until well blended. In medium bowl combine flour, cocoa powder, baking powder and salt; add to chocolate mixture. Stir in 1 cup "M&M's"® Chocolate Mini Baking Bits. Spread batter evenly into prepared pan. Bake 35 to 40 minutes or until toothpick inserted in center comes out clean. Cool completely on wire rack. Prepare Coconut Topping. Spread over brownies; sprinkle with remaining ½ cup "M&M's"® Chocolate Mini Baking Bits. Cut into bars. Store in tightly covered container. *Makes 16 brownies*

Coconut Topping

½ cup (1 stick) butter
⅓ cup firmly packed light brown sugar
⅓ cup light corn syrup
 1 cup sweetened shredded coconut, toasted*
¾ cup chopped pecans
1 teaspoon vanilla extract

*To toast coconut, spread evenly on cookie sheet. Toast in preheated 350°F oven 7 to 8 minutes or until golden brown, stirring occasionally.

In large saucepan melt butter over medium heat; add brown sugar and corn syrup, stirring constantly until thick and bubbly. Remove from heat and stir in remaining ingredients.

Coconutty "M&M's"® Brownies

Cranberry-Orange Snack Mix

2 cups oatmeal cereal squares
2 cups corn cereal squares
2 cups mini pretzels
1 cup whole almonds
¼ cup (½ stick) butter
⅓ cup frozen orange juice concentrate, thawed
3 tablespoons packed brown sugar
1 teaspoon ground cinnamon
¾ teaspoon ground ginger
¼ teaspoon ground nutmeg
⅔ cup dried cranberries or raisins

1. Preheat oven to 250°F. Spray 13×9-inch baking pan with nonstick cooking spray.

2. Combine cereal squares, pretzels and almonds in large bowl; set aside.

3. Melt butter in medium microwavable bowl on HIGH 45 to 60 seconds. Stir in orange juice concentrate, brown sugar, cinnamon, ginger and nutmeg until blended. Pour over cereal mixture; stir well to coat. Spread in single layer in prepared pan.

4. Bake 50 minutes, stirring every 10 minutes. Stir in cranberries. Let cool in pan on wire rack, leaving uncovered until mixture is crisp. Store in airtight container or resealable food storage bags. *Makes 8 cups snack mix*

Quick Apple Punch

4 cups MOTT'S® Apple Juice
2 cups cranberry juice cocktail
2 tablespoons lemon juice
1 liter ginger ale, chilled
Crushed ice, as needed

In large bowl, combine apple juice, cranberry juice and lemon juice. Fifteen minutes before serving, add ginger ale and crushed ice. Do not stir. *Makes 15 servings*

Kid Kabobs with Cheesy Mustard Dip

Dip
> 1 container (8 ounces) whipped cream cheese
> ¼ cup milk
> 3 tablespoons *French's*® Bold n' Spicy Brown Mustard or
>   Sweet & Tangy Honey Mustard
> 2 tablespoons mayonnaise
> 2 tablespoons minced green onions

Kabobs
> ½ pound deli luncheon meat or cooked chicken and turkey, cut into
>   1-inch cubes
> ½ pound Swiss, Cheddar or Monterey Jack cheese, cut into
>   1-inch cubes
> 2 cups cut-up assorted vegetables such as broccoli, carrots,
>   peppers, cucumbers and celery
> 16 wooden picks, about 6-inches long

1. Combine ingredients for dip in medium bowl; mix until well blended.

2. To make kabobs, place cubes of meat, cheese and chunks of vegetables on wooden picks.

3. Serve kabobs with dip.   *Makes 8 servings (about 1¼ cups dip)*

Prep Time: 15 minutes

Rock 'n' Rollers

4 (6- to 7-inch) flour tortillas
4 ounces Neufchâtel cheese, softened
⅓ cup peach preserves
1 cup (4 ounces) shredded fat-free Cheddar cheese
½ cup packed, stemmed and washed fresh spinach leaves
3 ounces thinly sliced regular or smoked turkey breast

1. Spread each tortilla evenly with 1 ounce Neufchâtel cheese; cover with thin layer of preserves. Sprinkle with Cheddar cheese.

2. Arrange spinach leaves and turkey over Cheddar cheese. Roll up tortillas; trim ends. Cover and refrigerate until ready to serve.

3. Cut "rollers" crosswise in half or diagonally into 1-inch pieces.

Makes 4 servings

Sassy Salsa Rollers: Substitute salsa for peach preserves and shredded iceberg lettuce for spinach leaves.

Ham 'n' Apple Rollers: Omit peach preserves and spinach leaves. Substitute lean ham slices for turkey. Spread tortillas with Neufchâtel cheese as directed; sprinkle with Cheddar cheese. Top each tortilla with about 2 tablespoons finely chopped apple and 2 ham slices; roll up. Continue as directed.

Wedgies: Prepare Rock 'n' Rollers or any variation as directed, but do not roll up. Top with second tortilla; cut into wedges. Continue as directed.

tip

Neufchâtel is a reduced-fat cream cheese with extra moisture for easier spreadability. Any reduced-fat cream cheese may be substituted.

Rock 'n' Rollers

Patriotic Cocoa Cupcakes

2 cups sugar
1¾ cups all-purpose flour
¾ cup HERSHEY'S Cocoa
2 teaspoons baking soda
1 teaspoon baking powder
1 teaspoon salt
2 eggs
1 cup buttermilk or sour milk*
1 cup boiling water
½ cup vegetable oil
1 teaspoon vanilla extract
Vanilla Frosting (recipe follows)
Chocolate stars or blue and red decorating icings (in tube)

To sour milk: Use 1 tablespoon white vinegar plus milk to equal 1 cup.

1. Heat oven to 350°F. Grease and flour muffin cups (2½ inches in diameter) or line with paper bake cups.

2. Combine dry ingredients in large bowl. Add eggs, buttermilk, water, oil and vanilla; beat on medium speed of mixer 2 minutes (batter will be thin). Fill cups ⅔ full with batter.

3. Bake 15 minutes or until wooden pick inserted in centers comes out clean. Remove cupcakes from pan. Cool completely. To make chocolate stars for garnish, if desired, cut several cupcakes into ½-inch slices; cut out star shapes from cake slices. Frost remaining cupcakes. Garnish with chocolate stars or with blue and red decorating icing. *Makes about 30 cupcakes*

Vanilla Frosting: Beat ¼ cup (½ stick) softened butter, ¼ cup shortening and 2 teaspoons vanilla extract. Add 1 cup powdered sugar; beat until creamy. Add 3 cups powdered sugar alternately with 3 to 4 tablespoons milk, beating to spreading consistency. Makes about 2⅓ cups frosting.

Patriotic Cocoa Cupcakes

Jingle Bells Chocolate Pretzels

1 cup HERSHEY'S Semi-Sweet Chocolate Chips
1 cup HERSHEY'S Premier White Chips, divided
1 tablespoon plus ½ teaspoon shortening (do not use butter,
   margarine, spread or oil), divided
   About 24 salted or unsalted pretzels (3×2 inches)

1. Cover tray or cookie sheet with wax paper.

2. Place chocolate chips, ⅔ cup white chips and 1 tablespoon shortening in medium microwave-safe bowl. Microwave at HIGH (100%) 1 minute; stir. Microwave at HIGH an additional 1 to 2 minutes, stirring every 30 seconds, until chips are melted when stirred.

3. Using fork, dip each pretzel into chocolate mixture; tap fork on side of bowl to remove excess chocolate. Place coated pretzels on prepared tray.

4. Place remaining ⅓ cup white chips and remaining ½ teaspoon shortening in small microwave-safe bowl. Microwave at HIGH 15 to 30 seconds or until chips are melted when stirred. Using tines of fork, drizzle chip mixture across pretzels. Refrigerate until coating is set. Store in airtight container in cool, dry place.

Makes about 24 coated pretzels

White Dipped Pretzels: Cover tray with wax paper. Place 2 cups (12-ounce package) HERSHEY'S Premier White Chips and 2 tablespoons shortening (do not use butter, margarine, spread or oil) in medium microwave-safe bowl. Microwave at HIGH 1 to 2 minutes or until chips are melted when stirred. Dip pretzels as directed above. Place ¼ cup HERSHEY'S Semi-Sweet Chocolate Chips and ¼ teaspoon shortening (do not use butter, margarine, spread or oil) in small microwave-safe bowl. Microwave at HIGH 30 seconds to 1 minute or until chips are melted when stirred. Drizzle melted chocolate across pretzels, using tines of fork. Refrigerate and store as directed above.

Picnic Pizza Biscuits

1 can (10 ounces) refrigerated buttermilk biscuits
1 pound hot Italian sausage, casings removed
½ cup chopped onion
½ cup sliced mushrooms
½ cup chopped green bell pepper
½ cup (2 ounces) shredded mozzarella cheese
¼ cup marinara or pizza sauce
2 tablespoons *French's®* **Honey Dijon Mustard**

1. Preheat oven to 375°F. Separate biscuits; pat or roll into 10 (4-inch) circles on floured surface. Press circles into 12-cup muffin pan.

2. Cook sausage in large nonstick skillet over high heat 5 minutes or until browned, stirring to separate meat; drain fat. Add onion, mushrooms and bell pepper; cook and stir 3 minutes or until vegetables are tender. Stir in cheese, sauce and mustard; mix well.

3. Mound filling evenly in biscuits. Bake 20 minutes or until biscuits are browned. Serve warm or at room temperature.   *Makes 10 servings*

Prep Time: 30 minutes
Cook Time: 25 minutes

Fruity Cookie Rings and Twists

1 package (18 ounces) refrigerated sugar cookie dough
3 cups fruit-flavored cereal, crushed and divided

1. Remove dough from wrapper according to package directions. Combine dough and ½ cup crushed cereal in large bowl. Divide dough into 32 balls. Refrigerate 1 hour.

2. Preheat oven to 375°F. Shape dough balls into 6- to 8-inch-long ropes. Roll ropes in remaining cereal to coat; shape into rings or fold in half and twist.

3. Place cookies 2 inches apart on ungreased cookie sheets.

4. Bake 10 to 11 minutes or until lightly browned. Remove to wire racks; cool completely. *Makes 32 cookies*

Tip: These cookie rings can be transformed into Christmas tree ornaments by poking a hole in each unbaked ring using a drinking straw. Bake cookies and decorate with colored gels and small candies to resemble wreaths. Loop thin ribbon through holes and tie ends together.

Reese's® Haystacks

1⅔ cups (10-ounce package) REESE'S® Peanut Butter Chips
1 tablespoon shortening (do *not* use butter, margarine, spread or oil)
2½ cups (5-ounce can) chow mein noodles

1. Line tray with wax paper.

2. Place peanut butter chips and shortening in medium microwave-safe bowl. Microwave at HIGH (100%) 1 minute; stir. If necessary, microwave at HIGH an additional 15 seconds at a time, stirring after each heating, just until chips are melted and mixture is smooth when stirred. Immediately add chow mein noodles; stir to coat.

3. Drop mixture by heaping teaspoons onto prepared tray or into paper candy cups. Let stand until firm. If necessary, cover and refrigerate several minutes until firm. Store in tightly covered container. *Makes about 2 dozen treats*

Fruity Cookie Rings and Twists

Honey Carrot Snacking Cake

½ **cup butter or margarine, softened**
1 **cup honey**
2 **eggs**
2 **cups finely grated carrots**
½ **cup golden raisins**
⅓ **cup chopped nuts (optional)**
¼ **cup orange juice**
2 **teaspoons vanilla**
1 **cup all-purpose flour**
1 **cup whole wheat flour**
2 **teaspoons baking powder**
1½ **teaspoons ground cinnamon**
1 **teaspoon baking soda**
½ **teaspoon salt**
½ **teaspoon ground ginger**
¼ **teaspoon ground nutmeg**

Cream butter in large bowl. Gradually beat in honey until light and fluffy. Add eggs, one at a time, beating well after each addition. Combine carrots, raisins, nuts, if desired, orange juice and vanilla in medium bowl. Combine dry ingredients in separate large bowl. Add dry ingredients to creamed mixture alternately with carrot mixture, beginning and ending with dry ingredients. Pour batter into greased 13×9×2-inch pan. Bake at 350°F 35 to 45 minutes or until wooden pick inserted near center comes out clean.   *Makes 12 servings*

Favorite recipe from **National Honey Board**

Honey Carrot Snacking Cake

Brontosaurus Bites

4 cups air-popped popcorn
2 cups mini-dinosaur graham crackers
2 cups corn cereal squares
1½ cups dried pineapple wedges
1 package (6 ounces) dried fruit bits
Butter-flavored nonstick cooking spray
1 tablespoon plus 1½ teaspoons sugar
1½ teaspoons ground cinnamon
½ teaspoon ground nutmeg
1 cup yogurt-covered raisins

1. Preheat oven to 350°F. Combine popcorn, grahams, cereal, pineapple and fruit bits in large bowl; mix lightly. Transfer to 15×10-inch jelly-roll pan. Spray mixture generously with cooking spray.

2. Combine sugar, cinnamon and nutmeg in small bowl. Sprinkle ½ of the sugar mixture over popcorn mixture; toss lightly to coat. Spray mixture again with additional cooking spray. Add remaining sugar mixture; mix lightly.

3. Bake snack mix 10 minutes, stirring after 5 minutes. Cool completely in pan on wire rack. Add raisins; mix lightly.   *Makes 12 (¾-cup) servings*

Gorilla Grub: Substitute plain raisins for the yogurt-covered raisins and ¼ cup grated Parmesan cheese for the sugar, cinnamon and nutmeg.

tip

Wrap each serving of snack mix in a sheet of colorful cellophane and tie the package with ribbon, raffia or yarn so the kids can take the treats home.

Brontosaurus Bites

Mini Turtle Cupcakes

**1 package (21½ ounces) brownie mix plus ingredients to
    prepare mix**
½ cup chopped pecans
1 cup prepared or homemade dark chocolate frosting
½ cup coarsely chopped pecans, toasted
12 caramels
1 to 2 tablespoons whipping cream

1. Heat oven to 350°F. Line 54 mini (1½-inch) muffin pan cups with paper baking cups.

2. Prepare brownie batter as directed on package. Stir in chopped pecans.

3. Spoon batter into prepared muffin cups, filling ⅔ full. Bake 18 minutes or until toothpick inserted into centers comes out clean. Cool in pans on wire racks 5 minutes. Remove cupcakes to racks; cool completely. (At this point, cupcakes may be frozen up to 3 months. Thaw at room temperature before frosting.)

4. Spread frosting over cooled cupcakes; top with toasted pecans.

5. Combine caramels and 1 tablespoon cream in small saucepan. Cook and stir over low heat until caramels are melted and mixture is smooth. Add additional 1 tablespoon cream if necessary to thin mixture. Spoon caramel decoratively over cupcakes. Store at room temperature up to 24 hours or cover and refrigerate for up to 3 days before serving. *Makes 54 mini cupcakes*

Mini Turtle Cupcakes

birthday cakes

Surprise Package Cupcakes

1 package (18¼ ounces) chocolate cake mix, plus ingredients to prepare mix
Food coloring (optional)
1 container (16 ounces) vanilla frosting
1 tube (4¼ ounces) white decorator icing
72 chewy fruit squares
Colored decors and birthday candles (optional)

1. Spray 24 (2½-inch) muffin pan cups with paper baking cups or spray with nonstick cooking spray. Prepare and bake cake mix in prepared muffin cups according to package directions. Cool in pans on wire racks 15 minutes. Remove cupcakes to racks; cool completely.

2. If desired, tint frosting with food coloring, adding a few drops at a time until desired color is reached. Spread frosting over cupcakes.

3. Use decorator icing to pipe "ribbons" on fruit squares to resemble wrapped presents. Place 3 candy presents on each cupcake. Decorate with decors and candles, if desired.   *Makes 24 cupcakes*

Surprise Package Cupcakes

Batter Up

5½ cups cake batter, divided
1 (15×15-inch) cake board, covered, or large plate
1 container (16 ounces) white frosting, divided
Orange and blue liquid or paste food colorings
1 miniature chocolate sandwich cookie

1. Preheat oven to 350°F. Grease and flour 2-quart ovenproof bowl and 8-inch round cake pan. Pour 3½ cups cake batter into prepared bowl; pour 2 cups cake batter into cake pan. Bake cake in bowl 55 to 60 minutes and cake in pan 20 to 25 minutes or until wooden skewer inserted into centers comes out clean. Cool 15 to 20 minutes. Loosen edges; invert onto wire racks and cool completely.

2. Trim flat side of bowl cake and top of round cake. Cut round cake into crescent shape to create rim of hat as shown in photo. (Save remaining cake for another use.) Place rim piece on prepared cake board. Place bowl cake next to rim cake to form baseball hat, attaching pieces with small amount of frosting.

3. Tint ⅓ cup frosting blue. Tint remaining frosting orange.

4. Frost rim of cap and bowl of cap with orange frosting. Place blue frosting in small resealable food storage bag. Cut tip off one corner of bag and pipe blue lines on cap as shown in photo. Open sandwich cookie; place half of cookie, filling side down, on top of hat. *Makes 14 to 18 servings*

tip

Food colorings are available in liquid and paste forms. Liquid colors are readily available in supermarkets. Paste colors, which are sold at specialty stores, come in a wide variety of colors and are well suited to use with foods that don't mix well with liquid. Both types impart intense color and should initially be used sparingly, a small amount at a time.

Batter Up

Giant Birthday Cupcake

**1 package (18¼ ounces) devil's food cake mix *without* pudding in
    the mix, plus ingredients to prepare mix**
¼ cup peanut butter
2 containers (18 ounces each) vanilla frosting, divided
    Construction paper or heavy-duty foil
    Fruit-flavored candy wafers or chocolate shavings
    Birthday candle

1. Preheat oven to 350°F. Grease and flour two 8-inch round cake pans. Prepare cake mix according to package directions. Bake about 30 minutes or until toothpick inserted into centers comes out clean; cool completely in pans on wire racks.

2. Remove cakes from pans. Place one cake layer on serving plate. Combine ¾ cup frosting and peanut butter in medium bowl. Spread frosting mixture over top of cake. Top with second cake layer. Frost top and side of cake with remaining chocolate frosting. Mound frosting slightly higher in center.

3. Cut 36×3½-inch piece of construction paper. Pleat paper every ½ inch. Wrap around side of cake. Place candy wafers decoratively on frosting. Decorate with candle.
Makes 8 servings

Slinky the Snake

2 (10-inch) bundt cakes
1 (40×20-inch) cake board, covered
2 containers (16 ounces each) white frosting
   Green food coloring
1 cup semisweet chocolate chips
   Red fruit roll-up
   Assorted candies

1. Cut each bundt cake crosswise in half. Position each half end to end to form one long snake shape as shown in photo. Place on prepared cake board, attaching pieces with small amount of frosting.

2. Tint frosting lime green. Frost entire length of cake with green frosting, spreading frosting about halfway down sides of cake.

3. Place chocolate chips in small resealable food storage bag. Microwave on MEDIUM (50% power) 20 seconds. Knead bag several times, then microwave 20 seconds more until chocolate is melted. Cut tip off one corner of bag; pipe diamond pattern on back of snake as shown in photo.

4. Cut out tongue and other decorations from fruit roll-up. Decorate face and back of snake with assorted candies. *Makes 32 to 36 servings*

Slinky the Snake

Carousel Cake

1 (10-inch) bundt cake
1 (10-inch) round cake board, covered, or large plate
1 container (16 ounces) white frosting
  Orange food coloring
  Assorted animal-shaped cookies
  Decorating gel (optional)
  Assorted candies and decors
  Paper Carousel Roof (instructions follow)
  Colored or striped drinking straws

1. Place cake on prepared cake board.

2. Tint frosting orange. Frost top of cake with orange frosting, allowing frosting to drip down side of cake.

3. Outline animal-shaped cookies with decorating gel, if desired; arrange cookies on top of cake. Press candies and decors lightly into frosting.

4. Prepare Paper Carousel Roof. Place straws around cake to support carousel roof; carefully set roof on top of straws.   *Makes 14 to 16 servings*

Paper Carousel Roof: To create carousel roof, cut out 7½-inch circle from 8½×11-inch sheet of construction paper. Cut one slit from outer edge of circle to center; tape cut edges together to form carousel roof. For a two-color carousel, cut a second 7½-inch circle from construction paper in another color and fold into 8 wedges. Carefully cut out 4 wedges; glue them onto first circle of paper so colors alternate (before cutting the slit and taping the edges).

Carousel Cake

Touchdown!

**1 (13×9-inch) cake
1 (19×13-inch) cake board, cut in half crosswise and covered,
    or large platter
2 cups prepared white frosting
    Green food coloring
    Assorted color decorating gels
1 square (2 ounces) white almond bark
2 pretzel rods
4 thin pretzel sticks
    Small bear-shaped graham crackers**

1. Trim top and sides of cake; place on prepared cake board.

2. Tint frosting medium green.

3. Frost entire cake with green frosting. Pipe field lines with white decorating gel.

4. Melt almond bark in tall glass according to package directions. Break off one fourth of each pretzel rod; discard shorter pieces. Break 2 pretzel sticks in half. Dip pretzels in melted almond bark, turning to coat completely and tapping off excess. Using pretzel rods for support posts, pretzel sticks for crossbars and pretzel stick halves for uprights, arrange pretzels in two goalpost formations on waxed paper; let stand until completely dry. When dry, carefully peel waxed paper from goalposts; place on each end of cake.

5. Meanwhile, decorate bear-shaped grahams with decorating gels; position cookies throughout field as desired. *Makes 16 to 20 servings*

Touchdown!

Fudgy Ripple Cake

1 package (18¼ ounces) yellow cake mix plus ingredients to prepare mix
1 package (3 ounces) cream cheese, softened
2 tablespoons unsweetened cocoa powder
Fudgy Glaze (recipe follows)
½ cup "M&M's"® Chocolate Mini Baking Bits

Preheat oven to 350°F. Lightly grease and flour 10-inch Bundt or ring pan; set aside. Prepare cake mix as package directs. In medium bowl combine 1½ cups prepared batter, cream cheese and cocoa powder until smooth. Pour half of yellow batter into prepared pan. Drop spoonfuls of chocolate batter over yellow batter in pan. Top with remaining yellow batter. Bake about 45 minutes or until toothpick inserted near center comes out clean. Cool completely on wire rack. Unmold cake onto serving plate. Prepare Fudgy Glaze; spread over top of cake, allowing some glaze to run over side. Sprinkle with "M&M's"® Chocolate Mini Baking Bits. Store in tightly covered container. *Makes 10 servings*

Fudgy Glaze

1 square (1 ounce) semi-sweet chocolate
1 cup powdered sugar
⅓ cup unsweetened cocoa powder
3 tablespoons milk
½ teaspoon vanilla extract

Place chocolate in small microwave-safe bowl. Microwave at HIGH 30 seconds; stir. Repeat as necessary until chocolate is completely melted, stirring at 10-second intervals; set aside. In medium bowl combine powdered sugar and cocoa powder. Stir in milk, vanilla and melted chocolate until smooth.

Fudgy Ripple Cake

Drum Layer Cake

1 package DUNCAN HINES® Moist Deluxe® Cake Mix (any flavor)
1 container DUNCAN HINES® Creamy Home-Style Classic Vanilla
   Frosting, divided
Green food coloring
Thin pretzel sticks
Candy-coated chocolate pieces
Lollipops

1. Preheat oven to 350°F. Grease and flour two 8-inch round cake pans.

2. Prepare, bake and cool cake following package directions for basic recipe.

3. To assemble, place half the Vanilla frosting in small bowl. Tint with green food coloring; set aside. Place one cake layer on serving plate. Spread with half of untinted vanilla frosting. Top with second cake layer. Spread green frosting on side of cake. Spread remaining Vanilla frosting on top of cake. Arrange pretzel sticks and candy-coated chocolates on side of cake as shown in photograph. Place lollipops on top of cake for "drumsticks."   *Makes 12 to 16 servings*

tip

For a brighter green frosting, as shown in photograph, use paste food colors available from cake decorating and specialty shops.

Drum Layer Cake

Your Move

 1 (9-inch) square cake
 1 (10-inch) square cake board, covered, or large platter
 1 cup prepared white frosting
15 square dark chocolate mints
 8 to 10 chocolate candies
 8 to 10 chocolate and white chocolate candies

1. Trim top and sides of cake.

2. Frost entire cake with frosting.

3. Place square chocolate mints in checkerboard pattern on top of cake as shown in photo.

4. Arrange candies on top of cake as desired. *Makes 10 to 12 servings*

Olympic Gold Cake

1 package (18¼ ounces) banana cake mix with pudding in the mix, plus ingredients to prepare mix
2 containers (18 ounces each) cream cheese frosting
2 cups chopped walnuts, toasted
⅔ cup semisweet chocolate chips

1. Preheat oven to 350°F. Grease and flour two 9-inch round cake pans. Prepare cake mix according to package directions. Bake 22 minutes or until toothpick inserted into centers comes out clean; cool completely in pans on wire racks.

2. Remove cake from pans. Place one cake layer on serving plate. Spread ¾ cup frosting over top of cake. Top with second cake layer. Frost top and side of cake with remaining frosting. Gently press walnuts onto side of cake.

3. Microwave chips in small resealable food storage bag 1 minute on HIGH. Cut off very small corner from bag. Pipe five Olympic rings and "Olympic Gold Kid" on cake. *Makes 10 to 12 servings*

Tip: To easily make Olympic rings, turn a 2-inch-wide round juice glass upside down and press into frosting five times in desired location. This will act as a stencil to make perfect rings.

Your Move

Cookie Sundae Cups

1 package (18 ounces) refrigerated chocolate chip cookie dough
6 cups ice cream, any flavor
1¼ cups ice cream topping, any flavor
Whipped cream
Colored sprinkles

1. Preheat oven to 350°F. Lightly grease 18 (2½-inch) muffin pan cups.

2. Remove dough from wrapper. Shape dough into 18 balls; press onto bottoms and up sides of prepared muffin cups.

3. Bake 14 to 18 minutes or until golden brown. Cool in muffin cups 10 minutes. Remove to wire rack; cool completely.

4. Place ⅓ cup ice cream in each cookie cup. Drizzle with ice cream topping. Top with whipped cream and colored sprinkles. *Makes 1½ dozen cupcakes*

tip

Serving individual cupcakes is a fun change of pace for a kid's birthday party.

Cookie Sundae Cup

Ponies in the Meadow

**1 package (18¼ ounces) cake mix, any flavor, plus ingredients to
    prepare mix**
1 cup flaked coconut
  Green food coloring
1 container (16 ounces) white frosting
  Pretzel sticks
2 small plastic ponies

1. Preheat oven to 350°F. Prepare and bake cake mix according to package directions in two 8-inch square baking pans. Cool in pans on wire racks 10 minutes; remove from pans and cool completely on wire racks.

2. Place coconut in small bowl. Add 4 drops green food coloring; stir until well blended. Adjust color with additional drops of food coloring, if necessary.

3. Tint frosting to desired shade of green with food coloring. Place 1 cake layer on serving plate; spread evenly with ½ cup frosting. Top with second cake layer; frost top and sides of cake with remaining frosting. Sprinkle coconut over top of cake.

4. Stand pretzel sticks around edges of cake to create fence; arrange ponies as desired. *Makes 9 to 12 servings*

Tip: Additional decorations can be added to the cake, if desired. Arrange candy rocks or brown jelly beans to create a path. Use the star tip on red or yellow decorating icing to create flowers in the meadow.

Ponies in the Meadow

fun party food

Smilin' Cookies

1 package (18 ounces) refrigerated sugar cookie dough
1 tablespoon plus 1 teaspoon finely grated lemon peel
   Yellow food coloring and yellow decorating sugar
¼ cup semisweet or milk chocolate chips

1. Remove dough from wrapper; place in large bowl. Let dough stand at room temperature about 15 minutes.

2. Add lemon peel and food coloring to dough; beat at medium speed of electric mixer until well blended and evenly colored. Wrap dough in plastic wrap; freeze 30 minutes.

3. Preheat oven to 350°F. Shape dough into 32 balls. Place 2 inches apart on ungreased cookie sheets; flatten into 1¾-inch rounds. Sprinkle with yellow sugar.

4. Bake 9 to 11 minutes or until set. Cool on cookie sheets 2 minutes. Remove to wire racks; cool completely.

5. Place chocolate chips in small resealable food storage bag; seal. Microwave on HIGH 1 minute; knead bag lightly. Microwave on HIGH for additional 30-second intervals until chips are completely melted, kneading bag after each interval. Cut off very tiny corner of bag. Pipe chocolate onto cookies for eyes and mouths.

Makes 32 cookies

Smilin' Cookies

Meteorite Mini Cakes

1 package (about 18 ounces) chocolate cake mix
1¼ cups water
3 eggs
⅓ cup vegetable oil
2 containers (16 ounces each) ready-made vanilla frosting, divided
   Assorted food coloring
1 bag (11 ounces) chocolate chunks

1. Preheat oven to 350°F. Spray 12 (2½-inch) muffin pan cups with nonstick cooking spray; set aside.

2. Combine cake mix, water, eggs and oil in large bowl; beat 30 seconds with electric mixer at low speed. Beat 2 minutes at medium speed. Divide batter evenly among muffin cups. Bake 20 to 25 minutes or until toothpick inserted into centers comes out clean. Cool cupcakes in pans on wire racks 10 minutes. Remove cupcakes to wire racks; cool completely.

3. Using kitchen scissors, trim cupcake edges to form rounded, irregular shapes.

4. Place 2 cups frosting in microwavable bowl; microwave 30 seconds on LOW (30% power) until melted. Tint as desired with food coloring. Drizzle cupcakes with frosting. Refrigerate cupcakes 20 minutes. Dot cupcakes with chocolate chunks to make meteor surfaces. Melt remaining frosting and tint as desired; drizzle over cupcakes until chocolate chunks are covered. Refrigerate until ready to serve.

Makes 12 servings

Meteorite Mini Cakes

Banana Split Shakes

1 small ripe banana
¼ cup skim milk
5 maraschino cherries, drained
1 tablespoon chocolate syrup
⅛ teaspoon coconut extract
4 cups low-fat chocolate frozen yogurt
Additional maraschino cherries for garnish

1. Combine banana, milk, cherries, chocolate syrup and coconut extract in blender; process on HIGH speed until smooth.

2. Add yogurt, 1 cup at a time; process using on/off pulsing action after each addition until smooth and thick. Divide among 4 glasses. Garnish with additional maraschino cherries. *Makes 4 servings*

Pizza Snack Cups

1 can (12 ounces) refrigerated biscuits (10 biscuits)
½ pound ground beef
1 jar (14 ounces) RAGÚ® Pizza Quick® Sauce
½ cup shredded mozzarella cheese (about 2 ounces)

1. Preheat oven to 375°F. In muffin pan, evenly press each biscuit in bottom and up side of each cup; chill until ready to fill.

2. In 10-inch skillet, brown ground beef over medium-high heat; drain. Stir in Ragú Pizza Quick Sauce and heat through.

3. Evenly spoon beef mixture into prepared muffin cups. Bake 15 minutes. Sprinkle with cheese; bake an additional 5 minutes or until cheese is melted and biscuits are golden. Let stand 5 minutes. Gently remove pizza cups from muffin pan; serve. *Makes 10 pizza cups*

Prep Time: 10 minutes
Cook Time: 25 minutes

Banana Split Shakes

Peanut Butter Bears

2 cups uncooked quick oats
2 cups all-purpose flour
1 tablespoon baking powder
1 cup granulated sugar
¾ cup (1½ sticks) butter, softened
½ cup creamy peanut butter
½ cup packed brown sugar
½ cup cholesterol-free egg substitute *or* 2 eggs
1 teaspoon vanilla
3 tablespoons miniature chocolate chips

1. Combine oats, flour and baking powder in large bowl; set aside.

2. Beat granulated sugar, butter, peanut butter and brown sugar in large bowl at medium-high speed of electric mixer until well blended. Add egg substitute and vanilla; beat until light and fluffy. Add oat mixture; beat at low speed until blended. Wrap dough in plastic wrap. Refrigerate 1 to 2 hours or until easy to handle.

3. Preheat oven to 375°F.

4. For each bear, shape 1 (1-inch) ball for body and 1 (¾-inch) ball for head. Place body and head together on cookie sheet; flatten slightly. Form 7 small balls for arms, ears, legs and nose; arrange on bear body and head. Place 2 chocolate chips on each head for eyes. Place 1 chocolate chip on each body for belly button.

5. Bake 9 to 11 minutes or until edges are lightly browned. Cool 1 minute on cookie sheet. Remove to wire racks; cool completely.   *Makes 4 dozen cookies*

Peanut Butter Bear

Breakfast Mice

2 hard-cooked eggs, peeled and halved
2 teaspoons low-fat mayonnaise
¼ teaspoon salt
2 radishes, thinly sliced and root ends reserved
8 raisins or currants
1 ounce Cheddar cheese, cubed or shredded
Spinach or lettuce leaves, optional

1. Gently scoop egg yolks into small bowl. Mash yolks, mayonnaise and salt until smooth. Spoon yolk mixture back into egg halves. Place 2 halves, cut side down, on each serving plate.

2. Cut 2 tiny slits near the narrow end of each egg half; position 2 radish slices on each half for ears. Use the root end of each radish to form tails. Push raisins into each egg half to form eyes. Place small pile of cheese in front of each mouse. Garnish with spinach leaves, if desired. *Makes 2 (2 mice each) servings*

Prep Time: 10 minutes

Clown-Around Cones

4 waffle cones
½ cup "M&M's"® Chocolate Mini Baking Bits, divided
Prepared decorator icing
½ cup hot fudge ice cream topping, divided
4 cups any flavor ice cream, softened
1 (1½- to 2-ounce) chocolate candy bar, chopped
¼ cup caramel ice cream topping

Decorate cones as desired with "M&M's"® Chocolate Mini Baking Bits, using decorator icing to attach; let set. For each cone, place 1 tablespoon hot fudge topping in bottom of cone. Sprinkle with 1 teaspoon "M&M's"® Chocolate Mini Baking Bits. Layer with ¼ cup ice cream; sprinkle with ¼ of candy bar. Layer with ¼ cup ice cream; sprinkle with 1 teaspoon "M&M's"® Chocolate Mini Baking Bits. Top with 1 tablespoon caramel topping and remaining ½ cup ice cream. Wrap in plastic wrap and freeze until ready to serve. Just before serving, top each ice cream cone with 1 tablespoon hot fudge topping; sprinkle with remaining "M&M's"® Chocolate Mini Baking Bits. Serve immediately. *Makes 4 servings*

Breakfast Mice

Spaghetti Cupcakes

8 ounces spaghetti, cooked and drained
4 eggs, slightly beaten
½ cup grated Parmesan cheese
¼ teaspoon ground black pepper
1½ cups RAGÚ® OLD WORLD STYLE® Pasta Sauce
2 cups shredded mozzarella cheese (about 8 ounces)

Preheat oven to 375°F. Grease 12-cup muffin pan; set aside

In large bowl, combine spaghetti, eggs, Parmesan cheese and pepper. Evenly press into muffin cups to form a "crust." Evenly top each cup with Pasta Sauce, then mozzarella cheese.

Bake 15 minutes or until bubbling. Let stand 5 minutes before serving.

Makes 8 servings

Prep Time: 20 minutes
Cook Time: 15 minutes

tip

For a fun twist, add faces using broccoli florets for hair, eyebrows or nose, pimiento-stuffed olive slices for eyes and pepperoni strips for mouths. Bake an additional 10 minutes.

Spaghetti Cupcakes

Kids' Quesadillas

8 slices American cheese
8 (10-inch) flour tortillas
½ pound thinly sliced deli turkey
6 tablespoons *French's*® Sweet & Tangy Honey Mustard
2 tablespoons melted butter
¼ teaspoon paprika

1. To prepare 1 quesadilla, arrange 2 slices of cheese on 1 tortilla. Top with ¼ of the turkey. Spread with *1½ tablespoons* mustard, then top with another tortilla. Prepare 3 more quesadillas with remaining ingredients.

2. Combine butter and paprika. Brush one side of tortilla with butter mixture. Preheat 12-inch nonstick skillet over medium-high heat. Place tortilla butter side down and cook 2 minutes. Brush top of tortilla with butter mixture and turn over. Cook 1½ minutes or until golden brown. Repeat with remaining 3 quesadillas.

3. Slice into wedges before serving.   *Makes 4 servings*

Prep Time: 5 minutes
Cook Time: 15 minutes

Kids' Quesadillas

Sleepover Cake

**1 package (about 18 ounces) cake mix, any flavor, plus ingredients
   to prepare mix**
1 container (16 ounces) white frosting
   Red food coloring
2 long cream-filled snack cakes
   Decorative sugar sprinkles
4 marshmallows
   Red and yellow decorating icing
   Assorted candies for decoration
4 chocolate peanut butter cups (milk or white chocolate)
   Red, black or brown licorice strips (optional)
2 packages (6 feet each) bubble gum tape (pink or green)
   Bear-shaped graham crackers

1. Preheat oven to 350°F. Prepare and bake cake mix according to package directions in 13×9-inch pan. Cool in pan on wire rack 10 minutes. Remove from pan to wire rack; cool completely.

2. Tint frosting with food coloring to desired shade of pink. Place cake on serving platter; frost top and sides with frosting.

3. Cut snack cakes in half lengthwise. Arrange snack cakes, cut sides down, evenly on top of frosted cake. Smooth frosting over snack cakes; sprinkle with decorative sugar sprinkles.

4. Flatten marshmallows by pressing down firmly with palm of hand. Arrange marshmallows at top of snack cakes to create pillows. Use decorating icing and assorted candies to create eyes and lips on peanut butter cups. Add licorice strips for hair, if desired; or use decorating icing to create hair. Place decorated peanut butter cups on marshmallow pillows.

5. Unwind bubble gum tape; arrange across cake at edge of peanut butter cups to form edge of blanket. Arrange second bubble gum tape around base of cake. Tuck bear-shaped grahams around blanket. *Makes 12 servings*

Sleepover Cake

Rainbow Pastel Parfaits

2 tablespoons pink decorating sugar
2 tablespoons green decorating sugar
2 tablespoons yellow decorating sugar
1 tablespoon strawberry gelatin powder (from 4-serving size box)
1 package (4-serving size) instant vanilla-flavored pudding mix,
    prepared according to package directions
1 package (4-serving size) instant lemon-flavored pudding mix,
    prepared according to package directions
1 package (4-serving size) instant pistachio-flavored pudding mix,
    prepared according to package directions
½ cup whipped topping

1. Spread decorating sugars on 3 small, separate plates. Wet rims of 8 parfait glasses with damp paper towel. Invert glasses onto plates of sugar and coat rims of glasses with varying colors of sugar. Set glasses upright on tray to dry.

2. Stir strawberry gelatin powder into vanilla pudding, one teaspoon at a time, until desired shade of pink is reached. Fill each glass about ⅓ full with vanilla pudding mixture. Add layer of lemon pudding and layer of pistachio pudding.

3. Top each parfait with a dollop of whipped topping and any remaining sugar sprinkles, if desired.   *Makes 8 servings*

Prep Time: 15 minutes

Rainbow Pastel Parfaits

Pizza Dippin' Strips

1 package (13.8 ounces) refrigerated pizza crust dough
15 thin slices pepperoni
1 cup shredded mozzarella cheese (about 4 ounces)
1 jar (26 ounces) RAGÚ® Organic Pasta Sauce, heated

Preheat oven to 400°F.

On greased baking sheet, roll pizza dough into 12×9-inch rectangle. Fold edges over to make ¾-inch crust. Bake 7 minutes.

Evenly top pizza crust with pepperoni, then cheese. Bake an additional 8 minutes or until cheese is melted. Let stand 2 minutes.

Cut pizza in half lengthwise, then into 1½-inch strips. Serve with Pasta Sauce for dipping.
Makes 16 strips

Prep Time: 10 minutes
Cook Time: 15 minutes

Cranberry Bog Gorp

¼ cup unsalted butter
¼ cup packed light brown sugar
1 tablespoon maple syrup
1 teaspoon curry powder
½ teaspoon ground cinnamon
1½ cups dried cranberries
1½ cups coarsely chopped walnuts and/or slivered almonds
1½ cups lightly salted pretzel nuggets

1. Preheat oven to 300°F. Lightly grease 15×10-inch jelly-roll pan.

2. Combine butter, brown sugar and maple syrup in large saucepan; cook and stir over medium heat until butter is melted and mixture is smooth. Stir in curry powder and cinnamon. Add cranberries, walnuts and pretzels; stir until evenly coated.

3. Spread mixture in prepared pan. Bake 15 minutes or until mixture is lightly browned.
Makes 20 servings

Pizza Dippin' Strips

Pumpkin Spiced and Iced Cookies

2¼ cups all-purpose flour
1½ teaspoons pumpkin pie spice
1 teaspoon baking powder
½ teaspoon baking soda
½ teaspoon salt
1 cup (2 sticks) butter or margarine, softened
1 cup granulated sugar
1 can (15 ounces) LIBBY'S® 100% Pure Pumpkin
2 eggs
1 teaspoon vanilla extract
2 cups (12-ounce package) NESTLÉ® TOLL HOUSE® Semi-Sweet
    Chocolate Morsels
1 cup chopped walnuts (optional)
    Vanilla Glaze (recipe follows)

PREHEAT oven to 375°F. Grease baking sheets.

COMBINE flour, pumpkin pie spice, baking powder, baking soda and salt in medium bowl. Beat butter and granulated sugar in large mixer bowl until creamy. Beat in pumpkin, eggs and vanilla extract. Gradually beat in flour mixture. Stir in morsels and nuts. Drop by rounded tablespoon onto prepared baking sheets.

BAKE for 15 to 20 minutes or until edges are lightly browned. Cool on baking sheets for 2 minutes; remove to wire racks to cool completely. Spread or drizzle with Vanilla Glaze. *Makes about 5½ dozen cookies*

Vanilla Glaze: COMBINE 1 cup powdered sugar, 1 to 1½ tablespoons milk and ½ teaspoon vanilla extract in small bowl; mix well.

Pumpkin Spiced and Iced Cookies

Barbecued Beef Sandwiches

3 pounds boneless beef chuck shoulder roast
2 cups ketchup
1 medium onion, chopped
¼ cup cider vinegar
¼ cup dark molasses
2 tablespoons Worcestershire sauce
2 cloves garlic, minced
½ teaspoon salt
½ teaspoon dry mustard
½ teaspoon black pepper
¼ teaspoon garlic powder
¼ teaspoon red pepper flakes (optional)
Sesame seed buns, split

Slow Cooker Directions

1. Cut roast in half; place in slow cooker. Combine ketchup, onion, vinegar, molasses, Worcestershire sauce, garlic, salt, mustard, black pepper, garlic powder and pepper flakes, if desired, in large bowl. Pour sauce mixture over roast. Cover; cook on LOW 8 to 10 hours or 4 to 5 hours on HIGH.

2. Remove meat from sauce; cool slightly. Trim and discard excess fat. Shred meat using two forks.

3. Let sauce stand 5 minutes to allow fat to rise; skim off fat.

4. Return shredded meat to slow cooker. Stir meat to evenly coat with sauce. Adjust seasonings. Cover; cook 15 to 30 minutes or until hot.

5. Spoon filling into sandwich buns and top with additional sauce, if desired.

Makes 12 servings

Prep Time: 20 to 25 minutes
Cook Time: 9 to 10 hours (LOW) • 4 to 5 hours (HIGH)

Barbecued Beef Sandwich

Pupcakes

**1 package (18¼ ounces) chocolate cake mix, plus ingredients to
    prepare mix**
½ cup (1 stick) unsalted butter, at room temperature
4 cups powdered sugar
¼ to ½ cup half-and-half or milk
Red and yellow fruit roll-ups
Assorted colored jelly beans and candy-coated chocolate pieces

1. Preheat oven to 350°F. Line 24 standard (2½-inch) muffin pan cups with paper liners.

2. Prepare cake mix and bake in prepared pans according to package directions.
Cool cupcakes in pans on wire racks 15 minutes. Remove from pans to wire racks;
cool completely.

3. Beat butter 1 minute in large bowl with electric mixer on medium speed until
creamy. Gradually add powdered sugar, beating until mixture is stiff. Beat in half-and-
half, 1 tablespoon at a time, until frosting is desired consistency.

4. Generously frost tops of cupcakes.

5. Cut out ear and tongue shapes from fruit roll-ups with kitchen scissors; arrange on
cupcakes, pressing into frosting as shown in photo. Add candies to create eyes and
noses.   *Makes 24 cupcakes*

tip

Send the leftover Pupcakes home with the party
guests. Wrap individual Pupcakes in cellophane or
plastic wrap and tie the packages with ribbon or
raffia.

Pupcakes

Golden Chicken Nuggets

1 pound boneless skinless chicken, cut into 1½-inch pieces
¼ cup *French's*® Sweet & Tangy Honey Mustard
2 cups *French's*® French Fried Onions, finely crushed

1. Preheat oven to 400°F. Toss chicken with mustard in medium bowl.

2. Place French Fried Onions into resealable plastic food storage bag. Toss chicken in onions, a few pieces at a time, pressing gently to adhere.

3. Place nuggets in shallow baking pan. Bake 15 minutes or until chicken is no longer pink in center. Serve with additional honey mustard.   *Makes 4 servings*

Prep Time: 5 minutes
Cook Time: 15 minutes

S'Mores on a Stick

1 (14-ounce) can EAGLE BRAND® Sweetened Condensed Milk
**   (NOT evaporated milk), divided**
1½ cups (9 ounces) milk chocolate chips, divided
1 cup miniature marshmallows
11 whole graham crackers, halved crosswise
**   Toppings: chopped peanuts, miniature candy-coated chocolate**
**   pieces, sprinkles**

1. Microwave half of EAGLE BRAND® in microwave-safe bowl at HIGH (100% power) 1½ minutes. Stir in 1 cup chocolate chips until smooth; stir in marshmallows.

2. Spread chocolate mixture evenly by heaping tablespoonfuls onto 11 graham cracker halves. Top with remaining graham cracker halves; place on wax paper.

3. Microwave remaining EAGLE BRAND® at HIGH (100% power) 1½ minutes; stir in remaining ½ cup chocolate chips, stirring until smooth. Drizzle mixture over cookies and sprinkle with desired toppings.

4. Let stand for 2 hours; insert a wooden craft stick into center of each cookie.
Makes 11 servings

Prep Time: 10 minutes
Cook Time: 3 minutes

Golden Chicken Nuggets

Tie-Dyed T-Shirts

1 package (18 ounces) refrigerated sugar cookie dough
6 tablespoons all-purpose flour, divided
Red, yellow and blue food coloring

1. Preheat oven to 350°F. Grease cookie sheets.

2. Remove dough from wrapper. Divide into 3 pieces; place in separate medium bowls. Let stand at room temperature about 15 minutes.

3. Add 2 tablespoons flour and red food coloring to dough in one bowl; beat at medium speed of electric mixer until well blended and evenly colored. Wrap in plastic wrap; refrigerate 20 minutes. Repeat with second dough piece, 2 tablespoons flour and yellow food coloring. Repeat with remaining dough piece, remaining 2 tablespoons flour and blue food coloring.

4. Divide each colored dough in half. Press together half of yellow dough with half of red dough. Roll dough on lightly floured surface to ¼-inch thickness. Cut dough with 3-inch T-shirt-shaped cookie cutter or make a pattern out of cardboard. Place cutouts 2 inches apart on prepared cookie sheets. Repeat with remaining dough, pairing remaining yellow dough with half of blue dough and remaining red dough with remaining blue dough.

5. Bake 7 to 9 minutes or until firm but not browned. Cool completely on cookie sheets.

Makes about 1½ dozen cookies

Tie-Dyed T-Shirts

Banana Bread Waffles with Cinnamon Butter

½ **cup unsalted whipped butter, softened**
2 **tablespoons powdered sugar**
2 **teaspoons grated orange peel**
¼ **teaspoon ground cinnamon**
¼ **teaspoon vanilla**
1 **package (7 ounces) banana muffin mix**
⅔ **cup buttermilk**
1 **egg**

1. Preheat waffle iron.

2. Combine butter, powdered sugar, orange peel, cinnamon and vanilla in small bowl; mix well. Set aside.

3. Combine muffin mix, buttermilk and egg in medium bowl; stir until just blended.

4. Spray waffle iron with cooking spray. Spoon ½ of batter (1 cup) onto waffle iron and bake according to manufacturer's directions. Repeat with remaining batter.

5. Spoon equal amounts butter mixture onto each waffle.   *Makes 4 servings*

tip

Waffle and pancake batter, whether made from scratch or from a mix, should be mixed only until just blended. The batter may have lumps remaining. Overmixing will make waffles tough.

Banana Bread Waffles with Cinnamon Butter

Hearty Chili Mac

1 pound 90% lean ground beef
1 can (14½ ounces) diced tomatoes, drained
1 cup chopped onion
1 clove garlic, minced
1 tablespoon chili powder
½ teaspoon salt
½ teaspoon ground cumin
½ teaspoon dried oregano leaves
¼ teaspoon black pepper
2 cups cooked macaroni

Slow Cooker Directions

1. Brown ground beef in large nonstick skillet over medium-high heat, stirring to separate meat. Drain fat. Add tomatoes, onion, garlic, chili powder, salt, cumin, oregano and black pepper to slow cooker; mix well.

2. Cover; cook on LOW 4 hours.

3. Stir in macaroni. Cover; cook 1 hour.   *Makes 4 servings*

Hearty Chili Mac

Crunchy Peppermint Candy Ice Cream

1¼ cups water
1 (14-ounce) can EAGLE BRAND® Sweetened Condensed Milk
(NOT evaporated milk)
2 cups (1 pint) light cream
½ cup crushed peppermint candy
1 tablespoon vanilla extract

1. Combine ingredients in ice cream freezer container; proceed according to manufacturer's instructions.

2. Garnish with additional crushed peppermint candy, if desired.   *Makes 1½ quarts*

Irish Flag Cookies

1½ cups all-purpose flour
1 teaspoon baking powder
½ teaspoon salt
¾ cup granulated sugar
¾ cup packed light brown sugar
½ cup (1 stick) butter, softened
2 eggs
2 teaspoons vanilla
1 package (12 ounces) semisweet chocolate chips
Prepared white frosting
Green and orange food coloring

1. Preheat oven to 350°F. Grease 13×9-inch baking pan. Combine flour, baking powder and salt in small bowl; set aside.

2. Beat sugars and butter in large bowl with electric mixer at medium speed until fluffy. Beat in eggs and vanilla. Beat in flour mixture at low speed until well blended. Stir in chips. Spread batter into prepared pan. Bake 25 to 30 minutes or until golden brown. Remove pan to wire rack; cool completely. Cut into 3¼×1½-inch bars.

3. Divide frosting among 3 small bowls. Tint one bowl frosting with green food coloring and the second with orange food coloring. Leave remaining frosting white. Frost individual cookies with three vertical strips, green on left, white in center and orange on right.
Makes 2 dozen cookies

Crunchy Peppermint Candy Ice Cream

Easy Nachos

4 (6-inch) flour tortillas
   Nonstick cooking spray
4 ounces lean ground turkey
⅔ cup salsa (mild or medium)
2 tablespoons sliced green onion
½ cup (2 ounces) shredded reduced-fat Cheddar cheese

1. Preheat oven to 350°F. Cut each tortilla into 8 wedges; lightly spray one side of wedges with cooking spray. Place on ungreased baking sheet. Bake 5 to 9 minutes or until lightly browned and crisp.

2. Meanwhile, brown turkey in small nonstick skillet over medium-high heat, stirring to break up meat. Drain fat. Stir in salsa. Cook 5 minutes over low heat.

3. Spoon turkey mixture onto tortilla wedges. Sprinkle with green onion. Top with cheese. Bake 1 to 2 minutes or until cheese melts. *Makes 4 servings*

Serving Suggestion: Cut tortillas into shapes with cookie cutters and bake as directed.

tip

In a hurry? Substitute purchased baked tortilla chips for flour tortillas and nonstick cooking spray. Proceed as directed.

Easy Nachos

Hawaiian Breakfast Pizza

2 teaspoons barbecue sauce or pineapple jam
1 English muffin, split in half and toasted
1 slice (1 ounce) smoked ham, diced
½ cup pineapple chunks
2 tablespoons shredded Cheddar cheese

1. Spread barbecue sauce over each muffin half; place on foil-lined toaster oven tray. Sprinkle ham and pineapple chunks over muffin halves; top with cheese.

2. Toast about 2 minutes or until cheese is melted.   *Makes 2 servings*

Note: To heat in a conventional oven, preheat the oven to 400°F; heat muffin halves on a foil-lined baking sheet for about 5 minutes or until cheese is melted.

Prep Time: 5 minutes

Colorful Kabobs

30 cocktail-size smoked sausages
10 to 20 cherry or grape tomatoes
10 to 20 large pimiento-stuffed green olives
2 yellow bell peppers, cut into 1-inch squares
¼ cup butter or margarine, melted
Lemon juice (optional)

1. Preheat oven to 450°F.

2. Thread 3 sausages, tomatoes, olives and bell peppers onto 10 (8-inch) wooden skewers.*

3. Place skewers on rack in shallow baking pan. Brush with melted butter and drizzle with lemon juice, if desired. Bake 4 to 6 minutes until hot.   *Makes 10 kabobs*

Soak skewers in water 20 minutes before using to prevent them from burning.

Tip: For younger children, remove the food from skewers and serve in a paper cup or on a small paper plate.

Hawaiian Breakfast Pizza

Witches' Brew

2 cups apple cider
1½ to 2 cups vanilla ice cream
2 tablespoons honey
½ teaspoon ground cinnamon
¼ teaspoon ground nutmeg

Process cider, ice cream, honey, cinnamon and nutmeg in blender or food processor until smooth. Pour into glasses and sprinkle with additional nutmeg, if desired. Serve immediately. *Makes 4 (6-ounce) servings*

Serving Suggestion: Add a few drops of desired food coloring to ingredients in blender to make a scary brew.

Hint: Reduce the fat in this tasty brew by replacing vanilla ice cream with reduced-fat or fat-free ice cream or frozen yogurt.

Prep Time: 10 minutes

Mummy Dogs

1 package (11 ounces) refrigerated breadstick dough
    (8 breadsticks)
1 package (16 ounces) hot dogs
    Mustard

1. Preheat oven to 375°F. Using 1 breadstick strip for each, wrap hot dogs to look like mummies, leaving one end of hot dogs uncovered. Place on ungreased baking sheet.

2. Bake 12 to 15 minutes or until light golden brown.

3. Place dots of mustard on uncovered hot dogs for eyes. *Makes 8 servings*

Mini Mummy Dogs: Use 1 package (16 ounces) mini hot dogs instead of regular hot dogs. Cut each breadstick strip into 3 pieces. Cut each piece in half lengthwise. Using 1 strip for each, wrap and bake mini hot dogs as directed above.

Witches' Brew

Backbones

4 extra-large flour tortillas
1 package (3½ ounces) soft cheese spread with herbs
1 bag (6 ounces) fresh baby spinach
8 ounces thinly sliced salami or ham
8 ounces thinly sliced Havarti or Swiss cheese
1 jar (7 ounces) roasted red bell peppers, drained and sliced into thin strips

1. For each tortilla, spread 2 to 3 tablespoons cheese spread almost to edge. Layer evenly with ¼ of spinach, salami and Havarti cheese. Place bell pepper strips down center. Tightly roll up; cut off and discard rounded ends. Repeat with remaining tortillas and filling ingredients.

2. Cut tortilla rolls into 1½-inch slices; secure with toothpicks. Refrigerate until ready to serve. To serve, remove and discard toothpicks; stack two or three slices on serving plate. *Makes 18 servings*

Little Devils

1 package (about 18 ounces) carrot cake mix
3 eggs
½ cup solid-pack pumpkin
⅓ cup vegetable oil
1 container (16 ounces) cream cheese frosting
Assorted Halloween candies, jelly beans, chocolate candies and nuts

1. Preheat oven to 350°F. Line 18 (2½-inch) muffin pan cups with paper liners.

2. Prepare cake mix according to package directions, using water as directed on package, and eggs, pumpkin and oil. Spoon batter into prepared muffin cups. Bake 20 minutes or until toothpick inserted into centers comes out clean. Cool in pans on wire racks 5 minutes. Remove cupcakes to racks; cool completely.

3. Frost cupcakes with cream cheese frosting. Let each guest decorate his or her own cupcake with assorted Halloween candies. *Makes 18 cupcakes*

Backbones

Green Meanies

4 green apples
1 cup nut butter (cashew, almond or peanut butter)
Almond slivers

1. Place apple, stem side up, on cutting board. Cut away 2 halves from sides of apple, leaving 1-inch-thick center slice with stem and core. Discard core slice. Cut each half round into 4 wedges using crinkle cutter. Repeat with remaining apples. Each apple will yield 8 wedges.

2. Spread 2 teaspoons nut butter on wide edge of apple slice. Top with another crinkled edge apple slice, aligning crinkled edges to resemble jaws. Insert almond slivers to make fangs.

Makes 8 servings

Blue Goo Cupcakes

1 package (18¼ ounces) white cake mix, plus ingredients to prepare mix
Blue food coloring
1 package (6 ounces) blue gelatin
Blue decorator icing

1. Preheat oven to 350°F. Line 24 (2½-inch) muffin pan cups with paper liners.

2. Prepare cake mix according to package directions. Add 6 drops blue food coloring to batter; adjust color as desired. Spoon batter into prepared muffin cups, filling ⅔ full. Bake according to package directions. Cool cupcakes in pans on wire racks 5 minutes; remove to wire racks to cool completely.

3. Meanwhile, combine gelatin and 1⅓ cups boiling water in small bowl. Stir mixture 3 minutes or until gelatin is completely dissolved. Freeze mixture 40 minutes, stirring often or until partially set.

4. Pipe ring of blue icing around edge of each cupcake. Spoon 1 rounded tablespoon gelatin mixture onto each cupcake. Serve immediately.

Makes 24 cupcakes

Green Meanies

Dripping Blood Punch

4 cups pineapple juice
1 cup orange juice
8 thick slices cucumber
2 cups ginger ale
Ice
8 tablespoons alcohol-free grenadine syrup

1. Combine pineapple juice and orange juice in large pitcher. Refrigerate until ready to serve.

2. Cut cucumber slices into shape of vampire fangs (see photo). Stir ginger ale into chilled juice mixture. Fill glasses generously with ice. Pour punch over ice. Slowly drizzle 1 tablespoon grenadine over top of each serving. Garnish each serving with vampire fang. *Makes 8 servings*

Dem Bones

1 package (6 ounces) sliced ham
¾ cup (3 ounces) shredded Swiss cheese
½ cup mayonnaise
1 tablespoon sweet pickle relish
½ teaspoon mustard
¼ teaspoon black pepper
6 slices white bread

1. Place ham in food processor; process until ground. Combine ham, cheese, mayonnaise, relish, mustard and pepper in small bowl until well blended.

2. Cut out 12 bone shapes from bread using 3½-inch bone-shaped cookie cutter or sharp knife. Spread half of "bones" with 2 tablespoons ham mixture; top with remaining "bones." *Makes 6 sandwiches*

Dripping Blood Punch

Quick Sand

¾ cup creamy peanut butter
5 ounces cream cheese, softened
1 cup pineapple preserves
⅓ cup milk
1 teaspoon Worcestershire sauce
Dash hot pepper sauce (optional)
1 package (7 ounces) refrigerated breadstick dough (6 breadsticks)
5 buttery round crackers, crushed
Cut-up vegetables such as carrots and celery, and fruit such as apples and pears, for dipping

1. Combine peanut butter and cream cheese in large bowl until well blended. Stir in preserves, milk, Worcestershire sauce and hot pepper sauce, if desired. Transfer to serving bowl or spread in 8- or 9-inch glass pie plate. Cover with plastic wrap; refrigerate until ready to serve.

2. Preheat oven to 375°F. Cut each breadstick in half crosswise; place on ungreased baking sheet. Make 3 slits in one end of each breadstick half to resemble fingers. Cut small piece of dough from other end; press dough piece into "hand" to resemble thumb. Bake 8 to 10 minutes or until golden brown.

3. Just before serving, sprinkle dip with cracker crumbs; serve with breadstick hands, vegetables and fruit. Garnish as desired.   *Makes 12 to 16 servings*

Quick Sand

kids in the kitchen

Sammich Swirls

1 package (11 ounces) refrigerated French bread dough
Salt-free seasoning mix (optional)
Yellow mustard (optional)
4 slices light bologna
4 slices reduced-fat provolone cheese
2 teaspoons grated Parmesan cheese

1. Preheat oven to 350°F. Roll out bread dough to 12×10-inch rectangle. Sprinkle with seasoning mix and dot with mustard, if desired.

2. Arrange the bologna and provolone cheese in alternating circles, overlapping edges to cover dough. Roll up lengthwise like a jelly roll; pinch seams shut. Place dough, seam side down, on baking sheet. Sprinkle with grated Parmesan cheese.

3. Bake 25 to 30 minutes or until puffy and browned. Using hot mitts, remove baking sheet from the oven. Let cool. Carefully, cut into 1-inch-thick portions. Serve warm or at room temperature.   *Makes 10 slices*

Sammich Swirls

Frozen Florida Monkey Malt

2 bananas, peeled
5 tablespoons frozen orange juice concentrate (do not thaw)
1 cup low-fat (1%) milk
3 tablespoons malted milk powder (optional)

1. Wrap the bananas in plastic wrap; freeze until firm, about 1 hour.

2. Break the bananas into pieces; place in a blender. Add the orange juice concentrate, milk and malted milk powder, if desired. Blend until the mixture is smooth; pour into glasses to serve.

Makes 2 servings

Prep Time: 5 minutes

kids' tip

Before using a blender, have an adult show you the safest way to use it. Always put the lid on the blender before turning it on. Never put your hand in the blender when it is running.

Frozen Florida Monkey Malt

Cherry Tomato Pops

4 pieces (1-ounce each) part-skim mozzarella string cheese
8 cherry tomatoes
3 tablespoons fat-free ranch dressing

1. Using a table knife, cut the string cheese in half lengthwise. Remove the stem end of each cherry tomato and gently squeeze out about ¼ teaspoon of the pulp and seeds.

2. Press one end of string cheese into the stem end of the tomato to make cherry tomato pop. Repeat with the remaining cheese pieces and tomatoes. Serve with ranch dressing for dipping.

Makes 8 pops

kids' tip

Have an adult help you cut out the stem end of the tomatoes with a sharp paring knife and squeeze out the seeds and pulp.

Cherry Tomato Pops

Chicken Strips in Bacon Blankets

¼ cup Dijon mustard
¼ cup maple syrup
¼ teaspoon chili powder
4 chicken tenders (about 12 ounces)
8 bacon strips

1. Preheat broiler. Stir together mustard, maple syrup and chili powder in medium bowl. Take half the mustard mixture and put it in a small bowl; cover with plastic wrap and save it for later.

2. Using kitchen scissors, cut each chicken tender in half lengthwise to make two thin strips. Place the strips on a large plate. Brush each chicken strip with the remaining mustard mixture. Wrap 1 bacon strip around each chicken tender.

3. Place chicken tenders, bacon ends down, on the rack of a broiler pan. Wash your hands with soap and hot water after touching raw chicken. Broil 5 inches from heat for 4 to 5 minutes. Using tongs, turn the chicken over. Broil 4 to 5 minutes or until bacon is crisp and chicken is no longer pink inside. To serve, dip the chicken strips in the mustard mixture you saved. *Makes 4 servings*

Tip: Ask an adult to show you how to use the broiler.

Chicken Strips in Bacon Blankets

Mud Cups

1 package (18 ounces) refrigerated sugar cookie dough
¼ cup unsweetened cocoa powder
3 containers (4 ounces each) prepared chocolate pudding
1¼ cups chocolate sandwich cookie crumbs (about 15 cookies)
Gummy worms

1. Preheat the oven to 350°F. Grease 18 (2½- or 2¾-inch) muffin pan cups; save for later.

2. Remove the dough from the wrapper; place it in a large bowl. Let the dough stand at room temperature for about 15 minutes.

3. Add the cocoa to the dough; beat at medium speed of electric mixer until well blended. Shape dough into 18 balls; press into the bottoms and up the sides of the prepared muffin cups.

4. Bake for 12 to 14 minutes or until the dough is set. Using hot mitts, remove the muffin pans from the oven and place them on wire racks; carefully, press down the center of each cookie with the back of teaspoon to form a cup. Cool the cups for 10 minutes. Remove the cups from the pans to the wire racks; cool completely.

5. Fill each cup with 1 to 2 tablespoons pudding; sprinkle with cookie crumbs. Add the gummy worms.   *Makes 1½ dozen cookie cups*

Tip: To make cookie crumbs, put the cookies in a large resealable food storage bag; seal the bag. With a rolling pin or meat mallet, pound the cookies until they form coarse crumbs.

Mud Cups

Breakfast Banana Split

1 banana
3 strawberries, cut into slices
¼ cup fresh blueberries
1 container (6 ounces) reduced-fat strawberry yogurt
1 tablespoon low-fat granola
1 maraschino cherry

1. Peel the banana. Place the banana on a cutting board; using a table knife, carefully cut the banana in half lengthwise. Place the banana halves in a serving dish, separating the halves.

2. Place half the strawberry slices and half the blueberries on the banana slices. Spoon the yogurt over the berries. Add the rest of the strawberries and blueberries; sprinkle granola over the top. Garnish with the cherry.   *Makes 1 serving*

Prep Time: 5 minutes

Breakfast Banana Split

Funny Face Pizzas

1 package (10 ounces) refrigerated pizza dough
1 cup pizza sauce
1 cup (4 ounces) shredded part-skim mozzarella cheese
   Assorted toppings, such as pepperoni slices, black olive slices,
      green or red bell pepper slices, mushroom slices
⅓ cup shredded reduced-fat Cheddar cheese

1. Preheat the oven to 425°F. Spray a baking sheet with nonstick cooking spray; save the baking sheet for later.

2. Remove the dough from the package; place it on a cutting board. *Do not unroll the dough.* Using a table knife, cut the dough into 4 equal pieces. Form each piece of dough into a ball by rolling between the palms of your hands. Pat each ball into 4-inch circle on the cutting board. Put the circles on the prepared baking sheet.

3. Spread ¼ cup sauce on each circle of dough. Sprinkle with mozzarella cheese. Decorate with toppings to create faces. Arrange Cheddar cheese to resemble hair.

4. Bake for 10 minutes or until the cheese is just melted and bottoms of pizzas are light brown. Using hot mitts, carefully remove the baking sheet from the oven. Cool 10 minutes before serving.   *Makes 4 servings*

Funny Face Pizza

Quick S'More

1 whole graham cracker
1 large marshmallow
1 teaspoon hot fudge topping

1. Break the graham cracker in half crosswise. Place half the cracker on a small paper plate or microwavable plate; top with the marshmallow.

2. Spread the hot fudge topping on the remaining half cracker.

3. Place cracker with marshmallow in the microwave oven. Microwave on HIGH for 12 to 14 seconds or until marshmallow puffs up. Remove from the oven, being careful not to touch the hot marshmallow.

3. Immediately place the remaining cracker, fudge side down, over marshmallow. Press top cracker gently to even out marshmallow layer. Cool completely.

Makes 1 serving

Tip: S'mores can be made the night before and wrapped in plastic wrap or sealed in a resealable food storage bag. Store at room temperature until ready to serve.

kids' tip

Always wait for the marshmallow to cool before eating this s'more.

Quick S'More

Super Peanut Butter Sandwiches

⅔ **cup creamy peanut butter**
2 **tablespoons toasted wheat germ**
1 **tablespoon honey**
8 **slices firm-texture whole wheat or multi-grain bread**
1 **ripe banana, sliced**
½ **cup cholesterol-free egg substitute**
⅓ **cup orange juice**
1 **tablespoon grated orange peel**
1 **tablespoon margarine or butter**

1. Combine the peanut butter, wheat germ and honey in a small bowl. Spread evenly on one side of each bread slice.

2. Place banana slices on top of the peanut butter mixture on four slices of bread. Top with remaining bread slices, peanut butter side down. Lightly press together.

3. Combine the egg substitute, orange juice and orange peel in a shallow dish. Quickly dip sandwiches into the egg mixture, coating both sides.

4. Melt margarine over medium heat in a large nonstick skillet. Cook the sandwiches until golden brown, turning once. Serve immediately.   *Makes 4 servings*

Prep Time: 15 minutes

Super Peanut Butter Sandwich

Tasty Tortellini Salad

8 ounces refrigerated reduced-fat cheese-filled tortellini or
    cheese-filled cappelletti
1 ½ cups broccoli florets
1 cup carrot slices
⅔ cup reduced-fat creamy Caesar salad dressing
½ cup grape tomatoes, cut in half
2 tablespoons sliced green onion
3 tablespoons toasted sunflower seeds or soy nuts

1. Cook the pasta according to package directions; drain in a colander. Rinse with cold water; drain well.

2. Combine the pasta, broccoli, carrots, salad dressing, tomatoes and green onion in a large bowl. Gently toss until mixed well. Cover with plastic wrap and refrigerate 2 hours. Sprinkle with sunflower seeds just before serving.

Makes 3 (1⅓-cup) servings

Prep Time: 15 minutes
Chill Time: 2 hours

kids' tip

Always have an adult help you cut up vegetables with a knife. To be safe when using sharp knives, place the vegetables on a cutting board. Never hold the vegetable in your hand and try to cut it.

Tasty Tortellini Salad

Easy Layered Bars

½ **cup (1 stick) butter or margarine**
1 ½ **cups graham cracker crumbs**
1 **can (14 ounces) sweetened condensed milk**
½ **cup coconut**
1 **cup peanut butter chips**
1 ¼ **cups crisp rice cereal**
1 **cup semisweet chocolate chips**
½ **cup candy-coated chocolate candy or baking bits**

1. Preheat the oven to 340°F. Lightly spray the sides of 13×9-inch baking pan with nonstick cooking spray.

2. Put the butter in a glass 2-cup measure; loosely cover with plastic wrap. Microwave on HIGH for 45 seconds to 1 minute or until the butter is melted. Carefully pour the hot butter into the prepared pan.

3. Sprinkle graham cracker crumbs evenly over the butter. Pour condensed milk evenly over the crumbs. Sprinkle with the coconut, peanut butter chips, cereal, chocolate chips and candies; press down gently on the candies.

4. Bake for 25 to 27 minutes or until the top just begins to brown. Cool completely in the pan on a wire rack. Cut into bars.   *Makes about 36 bars*

Strawberry Lemonade

1 cup fresh strawberries, quartered
4 cups water
1 cup fresh lemon juice (from about 4 lemons)
¾ cup sugar substitute

This recipe was tested with sucralose-based sugar substitute.

1. Place strawberries in a blender; process until smooth. Pour into a large pitcher.

2. Add water, lemon juice and sugar substitute to pitcher; stir until blended.

3. Strain strawberry seeds and pulp, if desired, by pouring lemonade through a strainer into tall glasses filled with ice. *Makes 4 servings*

Chocolate Peanut Butter Candy Bars

1 package (about 18 ounces) devil's food or dark chocolate cake mix *without* pudding in the mix
1 can (5 ounces) evaporated milk
⅓ cup butter, melted
½ cup dry-roasted peanuts
4 packages (1½ ounces each) chocolate peanut butter cups, coarsely chopped

1. Preheat the oven to 350°F. Lightly grease a 13×9-inch baking pan; save the pan for later.

2. Combine the cake mix, evaporated milk and butter in a large bowl; beat with an electric mixer at medium speed until well blended. (Dough will be stiff.) Cut the dough into 3 equal pieces. Place 2 pieces of dough in the prepared pan. Press the dough onto the bottom of the pan. Sprinkle the peanuts on top of the dough.

3. Bake for 10 minutes. Using hot mitts, remove the pan from the oven. Sprinkle with the chopped candy.

4. Drop the remaining dough by large spoonfuls over the candy. Bake for 15 to 20 minutes or until set. Carefully, remove from the oven; place the pan on a wire rack. Cool completely before cutting into bars.   *Makes 24 servings*

Chocolate Peanut Butter Candy Bars

Mexican Pita Pile-Ups

4 whole-grain pita bread rounds
1 cup cooked, diced boneless skinless chicken breast
1 tablespoon lime juice
1 teaspoon ground cumin
1 cup chopped fresh tomatoes
¼ cup chopped green bell pepper or jalapeño pepper
¼ cup fresh cilantro sprigs, chopped
1 can (2¼ ounces) sliced ripe olives, drained
1 cup (4 ounces) shredded reduced-fat sharp Cheddar cheese

Microwave Directions

1. Place the pita rounds on a cutting board. Top each pita with ¼ cup chicken; sprinkle chicken with lime juice and cumin. Top with tomatoes, pepper, cilantro, olives and cheese.

2. Place each pile-up in a quart-size resealable food storage bag; seal. Refrigerate until just before serving.

3. Place each pile-up on a microwavable plate. Microwave pile-ups, one at a time, on HIGH for 1 minute or until the cheese is melted. Let stand 2 to 3 minutes or until crust is slightly firm. *Makes 4 servings*

Note: This is a great recipe to make when you have left over cooked chicken.

Mexican Pita Pile-Up

Cinnamon-Raisin-Chip Muffins

¾ **cup all-purpose flour**
¾ **cup whole wheat flour**
½ **cup old-fashioned or quick oats**
½ **cup sugar**
¼ **cup toasted wheat germ**
1½ **teaspoons baking powder**
1 **teaspoon ground cinnamon**
½ **teaspoon salt**
¼ **teaspoon ground nutmeg**
1 **egg**
½ **cup low-fat (2%) milk**
½ **cup vegetable oil**
½ **cup raisins**
½ **cup mini chocolate chips**

1. Preheat the oven to 350°F. Grease twelve (2¾-inch) muffin cups or line them with paper or foil bake cups; save the muffin pans for later.

2. Combine all-purpose flour, whole wheat flour, oats, sugar, wheat germ, baking powder, cinnamon, salt and nutmeg in a medium mixing bowl.

3. Beat the egg in a small bowl. Add the milk and oil; mix with a spoon. Pour the egg mixture into the bowl with the flour mixture. Carefully, stir with a rubber spatula or wooden spoon until almost blended. (There will still be some lumps.) Add the raisins and chips; stir until blended. *Do not overmix.*

4. Fill the muffin cups ⅔ full with batter. Bake for 23 to 25 minutes or until a toothpick inserted into centers comes out clean. Cool muffin pans for 15 minutes on a wire rack. Remove muffins from the pan to the wire rack. Serve muffins warm or at room temperature. *Makes 12 muffins*

Cinnamon-Raisin-Chip Muffins

Bacon-Wrapped BBQ Chicken

8 chicken tenders (about 1 pound)
½ teaspoon paprika or cumin (optional)
8 slices bacon
½ cup barbecue sauce

1. Preheat the broiler. Line the broiler pan with foil; save the pan for later.

2. Place the chicken tenders on a large dinner plate; sprinkle chicken with paprika.

3. Wrap each chicken tender with a slice of bacon in a spiral around the chicken; place them on the broiler pan. Wash your hands with soap and water.

4. Broil the chicken for 4 minutes; using tongs, turn the chicken over. Broil for 2 minutes. Using hot mitts, remove the pan from oven. Brush the chicken with half of the barbecue sauce. Broil 2 minutes. Remove the pan from oven. Turn the chicken over; brush with the remaining barbecue sauce. Broil 2 more minutes or until the chicken is no longer pink inside. Serve warm. *Makes 4 servings*

Bacon-Wrapped BBQ Chicken

Springtime Nests

1 cup butterscotch chips
½ cup light corn syrup
½ cup creamy peanut butter
⅓ cup sugar
2½ cups chow mein noodles
2 cups cornflakes, lightly crushed
Jelly beans or malted milk egg candies

1. Combine the butterscotch chips, corn syrup, peanut butter and sugar in a large microwavable bowl. Microwave on HIGH for 1 to 1½ minutes or until melted and smooth, stirring every 30 seconds.

2. Add the chow mein noodles and cornflakes; stir until evenly coated. Quickly shape scant ¼-cupfuls of mixture into balls. Place balls on waxed paper. Make an indentation in the centers of the balls to make nests. Let the nests cool. Place 3 jelly beans in each nest.

Makes 1½ dozen treats

kids' tip

To crush the cornflakes, place them in a large resealable food storage bag; seal the bag. Roll a rolling pin over the bag two or three times or until the cereal is in medium pieces.

Springtime Nests

Pizza Rollers

1 package (10 ounces) refrigerated pizza dough
½ cup pizza sauce
18 slices turkey pepperoni
6 sticks part-skim mozzarella cheese

1. Preheat the oven to 425°F. Coat a baking sheet with nonstick cooking spray; save the baking sheet for later.

2. Unwrap the pizza dough. Roll out the dough on the baking sheet to form a 12×9-inch rectangle. Using a table knife, cut the dough into 6 (4½×4-inch) rectangles. Spread about 1 tablespoon sauce over center third of each rectangle. Top with 3 slices pepperoni and a stick of mozzarella cheese. Bring the ends of dough together over cheese, pinching to seal edges of dough and ends of the rollers. Place rollers, seam side down, on the prepared baking sheet.

3. Bake for 10 minutes or until golden brown. Using hot mitts, remove the baking sheet from the oven. Let the rollers cool for 5 minutes before serving them.

Makes 6 servings

kids' tip

You need to tightly seal the edges of the dough by pinching them between you thumb and first finger. Seal the ends of the rolls, too. If the seals aren't tight the cheese will run out of the rollers.

Pizza Rollers

Layered Cookie Bars

¾ cup (1½ sticks) butter or margarine
1¾ cups vanilla wafer crumbs
6 tablespoons HERSHEY'S Cocoa
¼ cup sugar
1 can (14 ounces) sweetened condensed milk
1 cup HERSHEY'S Semi-Sweet Chocolate Chips
¾ cup HEATH® BITS 'O BRICKLE® Toffee Bits
1 cup chopped walnuts

1. Heat oven to 350°F. Melt butter in 13×9×2-inch baking pan in oven. Combine crumbs, cocoa and sugar in a medium bowl; sprinkle over butter.

2. Pour sweetened condensed milk evenly on top of crumbs. Top with chocolate chips and toffee bits, then nuts; press down firmly.

3. Bake 25 to 30 minutes or until lightly browned. Cool completely in pan on wire rack. Chill, if desired. Cut into bars. Store covered at room temperature.

Makes about 36 bars

Layered Cookie Bars

Dessert to Go

1 (10-ounce) jar maraschino cherries
**1 (4-serving-size) package any flavor instant pudding (chocolate is
   good!)**
1¾ cups cold milk
3 cups whipped topping
6 flat-bottom ice cream cones
Colored sprinkles and/or maraschino cherries, for garnish

1. Put a colander or strainer in a small bowl. Pour cherries into the strainer, draining the juice into the bowl. You do not need the juice for this recipe; save the juice to add to orange juice or other drinks.

2. Put the drained cherries on a cutting board. With a sharp knife, carefully cut each cherry in half. *Have an adult show you how to use the knife.* Save the cherries for later.

3. Prepare pudding according to package directions using 1¾ cups cold milk. Refrigerate pudding 10 minutes.

4. Meanwhile, put the cherry halves in a large mixing bowl. With a rubber spatula, scoop whipped topping into the bowl. Stir gently until cherries are mixed with whipped topping.

5. Fill each cone with ¼ cup pudding. Top each with ½ cup cherry mixture. Decorate with colored sprinkles or a maraschino cherry. Serve immediately. This dessert is best eaten with a spoon.   *Makes 6 servings*

Favorite recipe from **Cherry Marketing Institute**

P-Balls

1 cup puffed rice dry cereal
½ cup cornstarch
½ cup peanut butter
¼ cup cold water
1 tablespoon chocolate chips
1 tablespoons sugar substitute

Mix all the ingredients together in a medium bowl. Form the mixture into 8 balls of equal size. Place balls on a plate; cover with plastic wrap. Refrigerate until ready to serve. *Makes 8 servings*

Crispy Bacon Sticks

½ cup (1½ ounces) grated Wisconsin Parmesan cheese, divided
5 slices bacon, cut in half lengthwise
10 breadsticks

Microwave Directions

Spread ¼ cup cheese on plate. Press one side of bacon into cheese; wrap diagonally around breadstick with cheese-coated side toward stick. Place on paper plate or microwave-safe baking sheet lined with paper towels. Repeat with remaining bacon halves, cheese and breadsticks. Microwave on HIGH 4 to 6 minutes until bacon is cooked, checking for doneness after 4 minutes. Roll again in remaining ¼ cup Parmesan cheese. Serve warm. *Makes 10 sticks*

Favorite recipe from **Wisconsin Milk Marketing Board**

acknowledgments

The publisher would like to thank the companies and organizations listed below for the use of their recipes and photographs in this publication.

Birds Eye Foods

Cherry Marketing Institute

Delmarva Poultry Industry, Inc.

Del Monte Corporation

Duncan Hines® and Moist Deluxe® are registered trademarks of Pinnacle Foods Corp.

Eagle Brand®

The Golden Grain Company®

The Hershey Company

The Hidden Valley® Food Products Company

Hormel Foods, LLC

Lawry's® Foods

© Mars, Incorporated 2005

MASTERFOODS USA

Mott's® is a registered trademark of Mott's, LLP

National Honey Board

National Turkey Federation

Nestlé USA

Newman's Own, Inc.®

Reckitt Benckiser Inc.

Riviana Foods Inc.

Sargento® Foods Inc.

The Sugar Association, Inc.

Reprinted with permission of Sunkist Growers, Inc.

TexaSweet Citrus Marketing, Inc.

Unilever Foods North America

Veg•All®

Washington Apple Commission

Wisconsin Milk Marketing Board

index

metric conversion chart

VOLUME MEASUREMENTS (dry)

¹/₈ teaspoon = 0.5 mL
¹/₄ teaspoon = 1 mL
¹/₂ teaspoon = 2 mL
³/₄ teaspoon = 4 mL
1 teaspoon = 5 mL
1 tablespoon = 15 mL
2 tablespoons = 30 mL
¹/₄ cup = 60 mL
¹/₃ cup = 75 mL
¹/₂ cup = 125 mL
²/₃ cup = 150 mL
³/₄ cup = 175 mL
1 cup = 250 mL
2 cups = 1 pint = 500 mL
3 cups = 750 mL
4 cups = 1 quart = 1 L

VOLUME MEASUREMENTS (fluid)

1 fluid ounce (2 tablespoons) = 30 mL
4 fluid ounces (¹/₂ cup) = 125 mL
8 fluid ounces (1 cup) = 250 mL
12 fluid ounces (1¹/₂ cups) = 375 mL
16 fluid ounces (2 cups) = 500 mL

WEIGHTS (mass)

¹/₂ ounce = 15 g
1 ounce = 30 g
3 ounces = 90 g
4 ounces = 120 g
8 ounces = 225 g
10 ounces = 285 g
12 ounces = 360 g
16 ounces = 1 pound = 450 g

DIMENSIONS

¹/₁₆ inch = 2 mm
¹/₈ inch = 3 mm
¹/₄ inch = 6 mm
¹/₂ inch = 1.5 cm
³/₄ inch = 2 cm
1 inch = 2.5 cm

OVEN TEMPERATURES

250°F = 120°C
275°F = 140°C
300°F = 150°C
325°F = 160°C
350°F = 180°C
375°F = 190°C
400°F = 200°C
425°F = 220°C
450°F = 230°C

BAKING PAN SIZES

Utensil	Size in Inches/Quarts	Metric Volume	Size in Centimeters
Baking or Cake Pan (square or rectangular)	8×8×2	2 L	20×20×5
	9×9×2	2.5 L	23×23×5
	12×8×2	3 L	30×20×5
	13×9×2	3.5 L	33×23×5
Loaf Pan	8×4×3	1.5 L	20×10×7
	9×5×3	2 L	23×13×7
Round Layer Cake Pan	8×1½	1.2 L	20×4
	9×1½	1.5 L	23×4
Pie Plate	8×1¼	750 mL	20×3
	9×1¼	1 L	23×3
Baking Dish or Casserole	1 quart	1 L	—
	1½ quart	1.5 L	—
	2 quart	2 L	—